LOPE DE VEGA

LOPE DE VEGA

MONSTER OF NATURE

By

ANGEL FLORES

KENNIKAT PRESS
Port Washington, N. Y./London

LOPE DE VEGA

First Published in 1930
Reissued in 1969 by Kennikat Press
Library of Congress Catalog Card No: 79-93062
SBN 8046-0675-7

Manufactured by Taylor Publishing Company   Dallas, Texas

" . . . and then appeared
the monster of Nature, the
great Lope de Vega . . . ."
MIGUEL DE CERVANTES

CONTENTS

ILLUSTRATIONS

LOPE DE VEGA

LEARNING TO WALK

TWO young men entered. The opening of the door let in no gust of wind, but the candles flickered.

"Good evening, gentlemen."

"Good evening."

The newcomers sat by themselves in a corner. Antón Cruz's tavern, the *Venta de las Animas,* was dark and musty. There was a penetrating, indecent smell of men and cider. Some muleteers were playing cards on a long, unpolished wooden table by the fitful, gossiping light of a candle. Some half-empty crocks presided over the game, quietly, like chessmen waiting for mathematical inspiration. On a stool lay a humped leather wine bag, like a sleepy dromedary. The cards, oily and obedient, moved

with silent resignation in the deft, conjuring hands
of these capricious somnambulists.

Antón came out of the adjoining chamber holding a candle.

"Good evening, gentlemen."

"Good evening."

"What can I do for you? "

"Bring us some sardines with onions, bread and
a few olives."

"And the best you have to drink."

"Yes, sir."

Antón left the candle on the table and went out.
The young men were tired and hungry. They remained silent until Antón returned with their order.
A cat approached, fixing his bright, scrutinizing
eyes on the lads. The first sardine from the earthenware plate went to the cat, as to a tutelary god to
whom homage was due.

"Caramba," cried one of the card-players, an-
noyed at having made a mistake. The cat looked
at him and his partners with scornful uncon-

cern, much as it might observe frozen fishes in an aquarium.

The young men ate voraciously and finally began to speak.

" I say, Lope, let's stay here tonight."

" What for? "

" I'm devilish tired and we're pretty far from Segovia."

" Come along, Hernando, don't be so lazy! We'll get there long before sunrise. There I'll buy a burro and 'twill be easy travelling."

" But look here, Lope, we've walked a good stretch today. They'll never overtake us now; we've thrown them off our track. Let's rest a bit! I don't like the idea of travelling at night."

" Very well, have it your own way. Let's ask the innkeeper whether he can put us up," and with that Lope clapped his hands.

Antón appeared immediately.

" Well, gentlemen? "

" Is there anywhere we can sleep? "

5

" Certainly! It will cost you two reals to sleep on the hay, and three in a bed."

" We'll take the hay."

From the adjoining room came the premonitory notes of a guitar, tuning up. Then a woman's voice broke into song, a deep, sad, dusky song. It drowned the sputtering candles, the persistent murmur of the oily and obedient cards. The cat yawned and fell asleep with the salty savor of sardines on its pink jaws. The sentimental notes drew fantastic arabesques over the taciturn room, sombered with music.

"Tomorrow we shall be warmed by sweet Segovian flesh, Hernando . . . How's that? Then by Las Banezas' wenches, then by Astorga's . . . and then, the world will be ours! You hear me? The whole universe will belong to you and to me. (Especially to me! . . .) "

Antón came in to see if the gentlemen were still thirsty. Lope ordered more cider, bid Antón ask the musician to approach . . .

The first time Lope and Hernando entered Segovia it was through the Puerta de Madrid; they had plenty of illusions and what they considered enough money, so they bought a burro. But weeks later they returned from Astorga minus the burro and with empty purses.

From Crows' Cliff they watched that ship with sails unfurled which is Segovia: with its two tall masts, the twin towers of the Alcazar, and its sharp keel, formed by the intersection of the two rivers beneath the lofty stone hull upon which the city rests.

Crows' Cliff is a lugubrious place, a rocky silence suspended over a dark, murmuring ravine. Criminals are thrown from it by the hand of Justice and the silicious needles of its sides have pierced the hides of many a man. A strong stench of carrion hovers over the vermilion blossoming, over the scarlet stalagmites of this cathedral of torture, crows' paradise.

"Come along, Lope, let's go back to Madrid.

7

It's a bore to keep up this kind of life. Our people will give us the devil, but they'll soon forget about it . . ."

"So you're in a funk, eh, poor little frightened mother's darling! You've sniffed it, eh, sniffed the smell of the stables, the bovine smell of the stables we call home. Bah, you're a jellyfish, Hernando! Shame on you! I can tell you this: if I had enough money to go on, I wouldn't stop till I got to the Indies, ay, to that brand new world full of thrills!"

"That's all very well. The Indies will do for the hardy, but not for us who like rugs and silks and luxuries. You know very well that we're not fit to fight the wild men who live there. Let other people get the gold, spices and perfumes for us."

"Well, what shall we do *now?*"

"I've got our last two gold pieces in my stocking. And then, let's see, have you anything we can pawn or sell? How about that chain around your neck?"

"I hate to part with that, Hernando; it's the last

thing my father gave me, a few days before he died."

"Oh Lord! I'm not blaming you, mind; but you must admit that's being sentimental! And it's not much like a chap who's burning to run off to the Indies with a pack of scoundrels."

"Very well, then, I'll give it up on one condition: that we buy a nice bouquet for that girl at the *Venta de las Animas* who played the guitar and sang with such feeling, whose flesh was sweeter than Málaga . . ."

"Oh stop, you make me sick! Devil take all the wenches! They enjoy us as much as we do them and they get paid for it into the bargain! . . ."

The Golden Lion was the best-known goldsmith's shop in Segovia. It supplied the ladies' boudoirs, the gentlemen's coffers and the clergy's vestries, with magnificent gold and silverware, with rare, precious gems. It housed a fantastic collection of polished medallions, shining plate, sword-hilts,

chalices, rings, chains, cups and vases. The poly-
chromy of scattered stones threw impossible rain-
bows upon battle scenes, falconries or Gothic stories
woven on the tapestries. And yet from this radiant
universe of sleeping suns and brilliant constella-
tions escaped a cruel smell of usury. The shop belonged to Maese León Henríquez, the Jew.

Lope and Hernando entered the shop with their
keepsake. Maese León approached them unctuously. A large diamond-studded platinum cross
hung from a hypothetical gold chain, half hidden
under his long, full beard. The glittering cross
epitomized Maese León's glamorous Christianity:
it strove to attentuate his pronounced Jewish fea-
tures and gestures, to silence the reverberating *Elohais Elohais* ever pressing to his thin lips, to conceal the seven-armed candelabra that dwelled
within his glassy eyes.

" Yes, Your Excellencies."

"Here, sir, is a solid gold chain. How much will
you give for it? "

" Whose is it? "

" It belongs to us," Lope told him.

" Where did you get it? "

" It was a present."

" Why do you want to get rid of it? " the old Jew asked.

" For the simple reason that the clink of shekels is music to our ears."

"Um . . ."

Just then a hippopotamus-like apparition entered the shop: it was old Fray Gerundio de Jesús.

" Is it ready, Maese? "

" Not quite, Your Reverence, but if you wish to wait . . ."

" How much longer will it take? "

" Oh, not very long."

"Very well, I'll wait."

Whereupon the good Friar ruffled the calm of a placid sofa with the huge mass of his blessed humanity.

Maese León went into the back-shop. Soon

11

afterwards one of his apprentices left hurriedly as if on an urgent errand. He returned shortly after accompanied by a constable. Maese León reappeared.

" Officer, these lads are trying to sell me a chain which they cannot recall having bought. So I thought it might be wiser to have the judge listen to their story. *The Golden Lion* takes no chances. We want only honest trade! "

Something half grimace, half question mark, disturbed the waxy horizontality of the constable's mustachios. He took the lads along with him.

When the trio had gone, Maese León turned with reassured complacency to Fray Gerundio. He was confident his manner, calculated to advance him in the good graces of the pious plesiosaur, had accentuated his Christianity and would thus bring him the patronage of more monasteries and churches.

" You see, Your Holiness, this is how we do business here. Honesty is our second name! "

From the velvet sofa came as an answer only a muffled rhythm like a distant, palpitating sea. . . . Fray Gerundio was beatifically snoring! . . .

High on the bench, sat Judge Don Pedro Ramírez, a bundle of black justice under the dusty pallor of the court-room ivory crucifix. Lope and Hernando were frightened. The atmosphere of the chamber pressed on them, clad them in a heavy coat of armor, stiffened their movements and their thoughts.

Don Pedro called on Lope.

" Young man, what is your name? "

"Lope de Vega."

" How old are you? "

" Sixteen."

"Where do you live? "

" In Madrid."

" Why are you here? "

" Because I didn't want to stay at home."

"Why not? " the Judge asked.

" Well, you see, Don . . . I mean, Your Honor

13

. . . my father died and my mother did nothing but weep all day long, and I thought it was high time for me to be off and find my place in the world."

"Who was your father? "

" Félix de la Vega Carpio, may he rest in peace! "

"What! So you're de la Vega's child, eh? I often went to your father's shop, young man; I used to enjoy his company and admire his embroideries. Real masterpieces, they were. God bless his memory.

"You were quite a precocious child, I remember; he often spoke of you: how you made verses long before you learned to write and gave your sweets to any boy who would take them down to your dictation. My lad, Madrid is the place for you! How much longer will you take to finish your studies? "

"Three years more, Your Honor, three too many."

"No, no, you're going straight back, Lope, you

understand? And no more foolishness! Who is this fine lad with you? ”

“A schoolmate of mine. We studied at the Jesuits’ and entered the University of Alcalá together. He is the famous Don Hernando Muñoz! ”

“Well, Hernando, you’re going straight back to Madrid with Lope and then to the University. Do you hear me? ”

“Yes, sir. We have been lucky indeed to have had you for a judge. Thank you, Your Honor.”

Don Pedro called a constable. He was to accompany them on horseback to Madrid.

Hernando heaved a sigh of relief; but down Lope’s cheek rolled an inexplicable tear. . . .

The Cathedral bells rang out across the air, summoning the people of Segovia to the burial of some hidalgo. Their plaintive dirge spread over the Castilian wasteland. . . .

15

II

ALMA MATER

LOPE was given a good scolding when he arrived at Madrid. His mother called him rebellious, ungrateful. " A few more shocks like this will be the death of me! Then maybe you'll be sorry for what you've done. But the worst of it all is that Don Jerónimo is terribly angry with you," she finished.

Don Jerónimo Manrique de Lara was Lope's protector. He was a very kindly old man; when they told him of Lope's escapade, he had merely smiled, for he, too, had sown his wild oats in his youth. People said that he was a staunch advocate of a higher census — he was the father of countless children and a good bishop in spite of it. His divinity was steeped in worldliness.

Don Jerónimo, who belonged to the noble house of the Counts of Paredes, numbered among his ancestors the stalwart knight and exquisite poet, Don Jorge Manrique. He himself had been vicar-general at Lepanto. In later years, he became Bishop of Cartagena, Bishop of Avila and Grand Inquisitor. He met Lope at the Jesuit School, fell under the spell of the precocious child, enjoyed his poetry and his ambitious translation of Claudian's *De Raptu Proserpinae.* So it was that he sent Lope to the University of Alcalá to study the arts and theology. Here the promising young poet decided to become a pope.

The University of Alcalá was founded by Cardinal Ximénez de Cisneros at the beginning of the sixteenth century. The Cardinal's idea of a university was somewhat radical for the Spain of that time. His emphasis was on the humanities: of the forty-two professorships, six were in Latin, four in other ancient languages, four in rhetoric and eight in philosophy. Civil law was not included in the curriculum, and only slight mention was made of canon law. The new institution attracted Spain's foremost scholars; learned men came to it from all the corners of the earth. The Cretan, Demetrios Dukas, came to Alcalá; Pincianus, the converts Alphonse of Zamora, Alphonse of Alcalá and Pedro Coronel, the great grammarian Nebrija, and the brothers Vergara, one of whom wrote the first Greek grammar to appear in Spain. The collaboration of all these men resulted in the magnificent *Polyglot Bible* (with Hebrew, Latin, Greek and Chaldean texts) completed in 1517.

In Lope's time, Alcalá was the proud rival of the famous University at Salamanca. Twelve thousand students sat on its painfully uncomfortable benches and listened to its lectures, with alert or soporific results. The student-body embraced a variety of intelligence as well as of background; every social class was represented. There were blue-blood aristocrats, clever rogues, serious-minded fools, noisy madcaps. In the sunny courts or in the shade of the

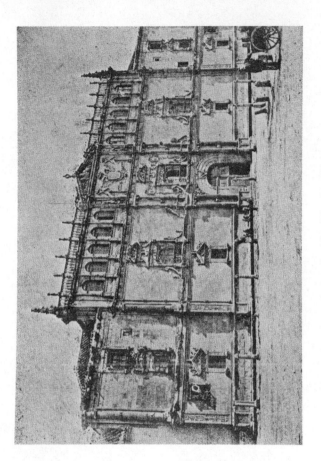

University of Alcalá de Henares

Mudejar amphitheatre one could hear a richly varied Latin, caressed by the linguistic peculiarities of various kingdoms.

Alcalá was a jolly college-town on the banks of the Henares river. Lope enjoyed life there because he felt free and because he was forever getting into trouble. He was a good-looking lad, tall, thin, swarthy and graceful. He had a somewhat long, hooked nose; his eyes shone brilliantly and smilingly, but they glittered with a malign flame when he became angry. He enjoyed enviable health and an enviable reputation for dancing, fencing, writing verse, borrowing money and telling " good ones."

Lope earned a few extra pesos at the Colegio de Santiago (a small school founded in 1550 by the Bishop García Manrique de Lara, a relative of Don Jerónimo) by doing a little tutoring. He spent all he earned and more. . . . There were plenty of parties too, and, besides, Alcalá was only a score of miles from Madrid. The tempting propinquity of the capital with its promise of easy incognito

escapades over the week-end hung over the students'
heads like a titillating sword of Damocles.

The richer boys lodged in private rooms and
cooked their own meals or went to the inn. But most
of the students were obliged to live in boarding
houses, where they must protect themselves against
the filching habits of chambermaids who were more
likely to clean out their trunks and coffers than to
sweep their dusty rooms. Not satisfied with the cus-
tomary meagre repasts that they inflicted on their
spiritual boarders, the landladies themselves were
always trying to add new fast days to the calendar.
Soup was a thin broth made from rancid bacon fat.
Salad was a world of wilted greenery, mostly radish
leaves, sprinkled with unsavory oil and sour vine-
gar. Meat pies were refuse-bones covered with
dough nicely baked. On Saturday came the inevi-
table tripe from unknown mammals and, on important holidays, a hodge-podge of boiled mutton,
mostly mammocks. For dessert, there were six
grapes or two apricots or a few raisins or perhaps a

thin slice of melon, depending upon the season. At times they tasted a transparent film of cheese whose texture, because of its infinite number of eyes, resembled the web wrought by a patient spider. On fish days, they had a dried salted pilchard served with head and all, or a stale addle egg. The bread was hard, the wine sour, but the stories and anecdotes were always well seasoned.

In order to get into the good graces of the landlady, one of the students would launch into a highfalutin' but facetious defense of longer studies and shorter dinners:

" Marcus Aurelius used to aver that only sots and fools had few books upon their shelves and plenty of meat upon their tables, stinting their minds more than their bellies, but that the wise man (proving therein his high wisdom) abhors full dishes and will feed very sparingly in order the sooner and the better to retire to his studies: that hogs' and horses' fatness did well become them, but that it was more commendable to be lean and slender, for

21

that your gross men are commonly gross-witted, they are unfit to fight for themselves or their friends; they are a kind of unwieldy lump, an unprofitable mass of flesh and bone, being not able to practise any manly exercise, whereas we see it is quite otherwise in those that are lean and not laden with fat."

Another student would then take the floor and answer: "I grant you that. But here is a more manifest truth, to wit: that a little meat or none at all quickly shortens the life of man. And if I may not live to thrive by my studies, it is but lost labor to drudge at my book. What falcon, I pray, was ever brought into the field to fly which was not first fed before it came there? What greyhound or other dog was ever put to course, or to hunt, before they had put victuals into its belly? They must both be kept reasonably high and not come hunger-starved into the field, for then will neither the one maintain its flight nor the other its course. They must be kept well fed and so must we students. There is a mean

22

in all things and that mean is the best. We will grant to these meat-moderators, these gut-mathematicians, that it is not meet to feed to surfeit nor to cram the belly to its utmost capacity, but we are not to fast until we grow so feeble therewith that our legs are not able to support our bodies or until our guts shrink and our excrement grows mouldy through the penury of our diet. . . ."

General applause followed and the lads at Alcalá made merry of their own hardships. They had come there to study the liberal arts and divinity, to qualify for the pulpit, to learn to say mass and to preach a sermon — a business which would assure their daily bread for the rest of their lives and nourishment for their own mortal bodies rather than enlightenment for their brethren's immortal souls. A few really did study, a great many gambled, but all sharpened their wits by trying to procure an extra morsel to better their slender and poor pittance. Their jewelry and their swords went with their Aristotles to the pawn-shops, A *Summae* visited the baker's, a Scotus often paid for a lamb chop.

Buxom witty wenches put hilarity into their evenings. There was music by the river and kisses in the alder groves. . . .

III

A HELEN AND A SIEGE

E mindful, O Lord, of Thy servants and handmaids who are gone before us with the sign of faith, and repose in the sleep of peace. . . . Incense rose in fleecy clouds. Hundreds of candles winked like so many sleepy stars. The dull buzzing of the Christian apiary anaesthetized the spirit. . . . *And repose in the sleep of peace.* . . . Elena Osorio always shuddered as she listened to the sad memento mori of the mass. With a venomous coldness, the funereal words entered her heart, penetrated the marrow of her bones. It made her feel like an ocarina ready to burst into sad music.

The idea of death terrified her. She remembered a child lying pale and rigid on an old mattress. She had seen the little corpse from an open window in the Alley of the Serpents. And there were many flies, jumping on top of each other, over the livid face . . . and this vibrating of tenuous wings across the immovable flesh that once ran and played and laughed in the olive-groves frightened her.

Then there were those two men stretched out on a beach, with a crowd looking on. It was long ago in a fishing village on the Cantabrian coast and she was only twelve. One man's breeches were torn; the crabs were making a meal of his genitals. The other fellow's eyes had been sucked out by octopuses. They smelled terribly, those two hidropic, tumorous, fish-eaten bodies lying on the sand among the seaweed and the seashells.

Again, more recently, as she was leaving for the country with her cousin, early in the morning, she had seen the pendulum-corpse of a peasant swinging gently in the morning breeze. The corpse hung from a torn and twisted tree, a tree gnawed and nipped and wasted as if by the sharp but patient claws of monstrous cats. An owl hooted from the lonely glen. Its note was sombre and pitiful, emanating, it seemed, from the thorax of the drying cadaver. And she trembled in terror at the twisted tree, at the hooting owl, at the protruding tongue, at the strange rustle of leaves in the dishevelled mane of distant branches. . . .

The organ heaved a last sigh of sacred music. The mass was over. A raucous clattering of chairs and benches. A shuffle of feet. Then an acolyte with his long pole extinguishing the sixty-seven candles on the high altar. The smell of the burnt candles mingled with the last tenuous clouds of incense.

Elena walked pensively, with painful hesitancy, towards the altar of Saint Margaret. She loved to look at that saint whom she called her Virgin of Smiles. The kind, young saint, beautiful, even somewhat coquettish, smiled from her gilded throne. Untouched by the funereal solemnity of the mass, she was like an affirmation of life. It was to a Virgin

27

like that Elena could confess her despair, her desire to live a more intense life.

Elena complained of her barren, uneventful existence. Her father, Don Jerónimo Velázquez, had guarded her zealously; she had a rather decent dowry (so he used to express it, quite proudly) yet there came to her from the sea of love only small ripples of flattery. Her suitors were unctuous actors playing the " gallants," diplomatically trying to get a better job in her father's company. She could recall no erotic thrills, no great anguishes of passion — only a little childish hugging, a little playful caressing, a few furtive kisses. Once, there was one long, long, warm kiss that she could recall. A young farmhand smelling of hay and the forest had once burned her month. . . . But, alas, that seemed ages ago! And then came her marriage. Marriage? Ha! Why call it marriage, that business transaction between her " benevolent " father, the actor Jerónimo Velázquez, and Cristóbal Calderón, the actor?

Don Cristóbal made a good fatherly husband. Courteous and obliging, though a little fussy. Sinapisms. Mustard-poultices. Rhetorical declamations. Rehearsals. Conservative habits. For three years she had been a faithful wife to a husband who spent most of his time away from home. *Faithful!* Foolishly faithful, alas, to a mummy! Was she to look forever into her cruel mirror, to mark the passing of time, the crumbling of her bloom, the flight of her dreams? . . . She, the futile Iphigenia, the excremental daughter of Jephthah!

Elena turned away from her Virgin of Smiles. She was a sad lady, tall and beautiful, pale, young, with clear, soft greenish blue eyes and long black eyelashes, walking along the black and white marble slabs of a solitary church.

An old vitrail rained soft purpurine rays of light into the font of holy water in which a hundred waterworms swam blissfully. As Elena bent to dip her finger into it she met a long, sensitive finger extended to offer her the precious liquid. She looked

29

up. A young man with a gentle but facetious and not quite holy smile stood beside her. He was a handsome Tobias with his finger outstretched as if pointing at some metaphorical fish. She accepted the holy water from him and crossed herself. They walked out of the church together.

An acolyte, spying from a confessional, burst into a torrent of none too catholic imprecations. The dark, silent dome re-echoed: " The lucky dog . . . that damned Lope! . . ."

Curtains hung in calm, lifeless rigidity, the carnations in the flower-pots listened drowsily, in blushing expectancy, but nothing stirred. In the streets, fans moved languidly and earthenware jugs, proud of the cold liquid in the generous frigidity of their bellies, were balanced carefully, on undulating hips or shoulders. The air only vibrated with the warmth of loud voices. But there was no wind, no breeze. The flaming sky of Madrid arched above like the gorgeous ceiling of some vast cathedral. Lope worshipped at the shrine of Elena's white young body.

A knock at the door; a servant cries warning. Don Cristóbal was returning. Lope half-dressed escaped through the window down a faithful rope that lay in wait under the bed like a serpent of safety. Through alleys and streets he would go, stop in at cheap taverns that echoed songs, loud voices and enraged curses, to recite poems dirty or bitter or crystalline according to his mood. According to his mood, too, he would spend the night at Paca's, Rita's or Milagros', or he would journey from Madrid back to Alcalá to attend an early class. . . .

Three summers went by; and life, even spent thus, can become dangerously tiresome. Besides, the sea is a lodestone to attract the restless hearts of restless men. . . .

Philip the Second, by the grace of God, King of Spain, decided to be King of Portugal and straightway accomplished his purpose. There was a certain

Dom Antonio who claimed that he was rightful heir to the Portuguese crown. " If I cannot be King of Portugal," he said, " I shall be King of the Azores."

The Azores were more precious in the age of swords and sails, when seas were wider. Spanish galleons homeward bound, rich with the gold from the Indies, had to pass near them. The islanders and other enemies of Spain skinned their fat prey upon those basalt cliffs. In short, the Azores were a thorn in the Spanish-lion's paw.

Dom Antonio went about Europe telling everybody how miserable he felt without his Portuguese crown. In France he found very sympathetic friends in Henry the Third and Catherine de Medici. They promised to help him. They were, of course, no philanthropists: what they really wanted was to poison Philip's life and to win a goodish share of booty from Portugal's immense coffer, Brazil. Dom Antonio next moved to England with his jeremiad. Elizabeth consoled him with pretty prom-

Philip the Second

ises, and to please him, she even consented to accept his gifts, and the diamonds from the crown of Portugal passed one by one into her dainty hands.

During the summer of 1582 the Azores were filled with Catherine's men. They challenged Philip. The Spanish monarch sent down that hardy rough-weather sailor, Alvaro de Bazán, an old sea-wolf with a beard grown gray with gun-powder and brine. No man had ever dared to tear his flag from the masthead. His husky voice had thundered above the cataclysmal alarum of Lepanto when John of Austria humbled the Turks and Cervantes lost his arm. He was politely avoided by French corsairs, English privateers and Turkish galliasses. But he bowed to the genius of Sir Francis Drake.

Don Alvaro crushed the Portuguese-French strength. And, alas, blessèd old Brântome's Friend, Philippe de Strozzi, was among the dead. It was a horrible nightmare of blood and suffering. When the Spaniards departed, the Azores lay on the restless sea and a stench of tragic shambles hovered over the slightly dilapidated walls of the island.

Scarcely had a year gone by when Catherine sent a fresh reinforcement of French troops. Monsieur de Chatres sailed from Havre on May 17th, 1583, in command of fourteen galleons that bore two thousand soldiers and a hundred pieces of artillery. Rumor had it that Sir Francis Drake was rushing from the golden seas of the west with his *Pelican* and many bold buccaneers.

Early on the morning of June 23rd, Cardinal Alberto gave his blessing to Don Alvaro de Bazán, to his 11,441 men in the ninety-eight vessels anchored at Lisbon. A young man knelt down and prayed. He felt the solemnity of the moment more intensely than the scarred, battered sea-warriors around him. His name was Lope de Vega; he was twenty-one.

The sea was a crystal xylophone with a green-blue motif. The foam dried its whiteness on the rocks. The wind barked among the caves, frolicked among pennants and flags, sang in the rigging of ships, filled wide anxious sails with favorable speed.

Twelve fast galleons were sent ahead. They arrived ten days before the rest, but two had to return home: the *Santa María de Socorro* with her hull sorely damaged on the reefs of Cachopos, and the *Santa María de la Costa* with a broken helm.

On July 23rd Don Alvaro sent trumpeters and some of his own Portuguese soldiers with terms of amnesty. The enemy refused to listen. At midnight two of Don Alvaro's galleons opened fire on the town of Praya. He was attempting to bewilder the enemy. Tenders, pinnaces and barges were lowered. Don Alvaro's troops landed near Porto das Moas. Two French forces and two Portuguese faced the Spaniards. There was rough and bitter fighting. The Portuguese Captain Brancino was killed. The Spaniards marched forward bravely, but Monsieur

35

de Chatres had been signalled; he arrived with his Frenchmen, and the Viceroy Manuel da Silva hurried up with his Portuguese. The battle lasted sixteen hours. The prize at stake was a little spring of cool water. It was a hot day — the soldiers were parched, the Spaniards had had nothing to drink. Spurred by a terrible thirst, they fought on. Among the bravest of the brave was a Spaniard named Rodrigo de Cervantes. He was the brother of Miguel de Cervantes!

Next day the Spaniards had the choice of drinking or dying. So they fought on fiercely and they won, but Don Alvaro would not allow them to drink until they had hoisted the Spanish flag upon the topmost tower of Angra. The Spaniards captured San Sebastián; Da Silva took to his heels, his men routed. Monsieur de Chatres retreated in good formation towards the Guadalupe mountain. The Spaniards captured Angra and drank plenty of fresh water; the Spanish fleet captured thirty vessels and ninety-one pieces of artillery, the Spanish troops forty-four forts and three hundred pieces of artillery.

Don Alvaro sent Don Pedro de Toledo and Miguel de Oquendo to capture the island of Fayal. On July 31st, Don Pedro dispatched a messenger with his edicts of surrender. The Governor at Fayal killed the Spanish envoy with his own sword. Next day the Spaniards landed at Feiteras and fought a bloody battle. After he had surrendered six flags and sixteen pieces of artillery, the Governor was seized, his hand was cut off and he was hanged from a fort.

Meanwhile, Monsieur de Chatres likewise surrendered to Don Alvaro flags, drums, fifes, muskets, arquebuses and pikes. He and his men were embarked in three vessels and sent home.

The " supple, inefficient and truculent " Viceroy, Manuel da Silva, had hopes of getting out of this mess. They found him hiding in the woods, waiting for a friendly boat to rescue him. Many a secret was wrung from him by torture; then, from the

37

rack they took him to the scaffold. His severed head was placed in the iron cage in which he had been accustomed to keep the Spaniards' heads.

A German hangman was kept busy for a few days. The islands reeked with blood. The odor of death was stronger than that of the fertile fields, of the briny sea.

On August 9th, Don Alvaro wrote a letter to Philip asking his permission to add England to his dominions. It was high time to punish " that troublesome Jezebel " Elizabeth. The Low Countries would then surrender forever. His Christian soldiers and his Christian fleet were ready and anxious for new conquests.

There was nothing new in Don Alvaro's suggestion. The Duke of Alva, Don John of Austria and the Duke of Guise had dreamed of the enterprise in past years. But never was the dream so well founded, so near its realization. Elizabeth trembled when she heard the news, and Drake burned a few towns in the Indies. Unfortunately Philip hesitated, sounded pessimistic notes. . . . And he thanked Don Alvaro for his kind words!

Don Juan de Urbina became Governor of the Azores. The Spanish flags waved proudly over the island and Spanish galleons could now stop to rest on their perilous journeys from America.

After twenty-seven days of choppy seas and storms, Lope landed in Cádiz, on September 13th, with the gaiety and assurance of a conqueror whose task is successfully completed. On his three months leave of absence from Madrid he had breathed the invigorating brine of rough seas and rough men and he had learned the secret of winning a fight.

Don Alvaro was not required to doff his hat in the presence of his king when he told the story of his victory. Philip named him Captain-General of the Ocean. There were bulls and cane tourneys, dancing and clowning in Madrid, and in the Royal Monastery of the Escorial the *Te Deum* was sung thrice.

IV

STABILITY, THY NAME IS WOMAN

LOPE stayed in Madrid. As secretary to the Marquis de las Navas, his repasts were excellent; his wines were of fantastic vintage; his writings exuded a healthy optimism.

In the spring of 1585 a poorly fed devil — Cervantes — published a pastoral romance entitled *Galatea*. At the end of the volume he dedicated a stanza in praise of each of the most distinguished of his contemporaries. One of them read:

" Wisdom and experience may make their home
  With the fresh green sapling years of untaught
     youth
  Exactly as they can with the grey hairs
  And ripened stalwart age that stand for truth.

I will argue with no one at all who tries to deny
This verity, self-evident and plain,
He must admit it so, and especially
When you, O Lope de Vega, are my refrain!"

As Lope soared towards Parnassus, he was fast losing his Helen. Elena believed that literary men talked and wrote entirely too much.

"You must not come tomorrow night, dear."

"Why not?"

"You see, the whole town is talking about us. My mother has been scolding me again. She slapped me across the face and tore a lot of hair from my poor head. You ought to see her when she gets angry — She's a wild cat, a perfect fiend!"

"The wretch! Why don't you tell her to mind her own business? Why don't you tell her that if I hadn't been writing plays one night after the other, her husband would have starved long ago? I have known you for years, and your mother, the excellent Doña Inés Osorio, owes me still more."

41

"But, dear, it's your own fault. You keep on writing about our love-affair."

"Isn't that the stuff great poetry is made of?"

"Why don't you follow Virgil and write about arms and the man? You've been to war, haven't you?"

"*Las cuatro en punto y sereno-o-o*" — "Four o'clock and all's well." The watchman's voice rose from the dark night like a psalm's soft tone. As he walked along his keys' metallic sound marked the slow cadence of his step. In the music of these long, heavy, complicated keys and in the rhythmic sound of the watchman's staff on the stones of the streets and alleys was a message of security, of restful shadows, of darkness shut in houses, of doors resting safely on strong hinges, while along the streets were men to count the hours, read the clouds and stars, and with metallic keys play fugues of calm.

Lope was not hearing Elena's words. His hand fell away from her warm breasts. He listened to the keys . . . they brought him a breath of the night air, of open spaces, a music of cowbells at sunset, a world of sheep-herds in movement, free, challenging the wolves, challenging the weather. He wished he were a black buck — no, not a black — rather a tall white unicorn, ringing its bell of freedom over the mountains, over the plains, towards the sea. A white unicorn singing a white hymn of purity and chastity to the Immaculate Lady of the White Lilies . . .

But the keys and the sounding staff were swallowed up in the long, dark silence of the night, and Lope felt again the softness of his pillow, and the mattress, and the red smell of sex. He placed his hand once more on Elena's burning breasts. His volcanic blood boiled with passion and he tried to crush Elena's beauty in the orgiastic embrace of his voluptuousness.

But there was to appear a powerful pretender to Elena's tempestuous bed. His eloquent attraction lay in his titles, his coat-of-arms, the ringing of his golden coins. He was a nobleman; he was rich. Elena's mother, the experienced Doña Inés, approved his qualifications beyond words. She was overwhelmed by the thought that His Excellency Don Francisco Perrenot de Grandevelle, Count of Contecroix, Chevalier of Alcántara, was having an affair with her daughter.

Lope had met Perrenot during the Azores campaign. In the course of their long conversations about classics, the stage, politics and women, Lope had glamorously painted Elena's portrait. He had praised her beauty, her grace, her cleverness, her talent as a dancer, as a singer, as a player of various musical instruments.

He succeeded in making the Count fall in love with her before even he had seen her!

Doña Inés became Elena's unremitting counsellor:

"You see, my child, it pays to be wise, then you will have nothing to regret in life. You know that the

Count is mad about you. And he is such a gentle-
man. When he gives you a flower, ask for a vase;
and when the vase comes, ask for a table; and when
the table comes, ask for a rug or a table-cloth. Or a
carriage, or a house. Day by day you must get
something more worth while. That's the word! You
hear me? — *worth while!* He's such an elegant
fellow! You can't imagine how proud I feel in having the little girl I bore under here, under my
heart, now in the arms of no less a personage than
the son of Philip the Second's Ambassador to the
French court . . . the son of the blessed man
whose bread no less a man than Maximilian the
Second of Austria deigned to butter. . . ."

Perrenot's rise to Elena's couch was phenome-
nally rapid.

And a new ex-voto was added at the altar of
Saint Margaret, in ivory and gold, with rococo
blue lettering: "*I adore you. You have made me
very happy, Holy Virgin. Thank you.*" A profusion
of artistically wrought candles stood round the

altar. Elena was very happy. She had a husband, a poet, and a Count.

Lope, for his part, had tired of Elena. As long as he was a student at Alcalá, this love affair in Madrid possessed the piquancy of adventure, kept him in constant danger, in melodramatic suspense, made his studies warm with sex. His imagination saw Elena's eyes charged with red flashes of complicated perversity. He felt he was playing a thrilling rôle in an intensely passionate drama.

When the gilt of adventure was dulled he went to Elena's room only through habit. She was a novel read. Her body dragged on him. He wanted to wring romance by the neck.

Now of course, with the appearance of a rival — and what a rival! — once again he took interest in providing this act of his life with a more glamorous anticlimax. He even declined to accompany his master, the Marquis de las Navas, on an excursion to Alcántara. He shut himself up at his mother's to write poetry. His pride was hurt. He was an egoistic Don

Juan, always aware of the fact that he was handsome, that he was a scholar, that he was a military hero, that he was a successful playwright, that many women were pining away with hopeless love for him. And therefore he felt that Elena ought to love him still. Gall boiled in the marrow of his bones and bile in his soul. He exploded in venomous verse.

In Madrid, this twenty-ninth day of the month of December in the year of Our Lord 1587, appeared before this Tribunal:

Rodrigo de Saavedra, about twenty-eight, of this city, living in the house of the widow Merchan at Relatores Street, who declared that he saw two sheets of paper, on which papers were written two poems: one in Latin macaronic verse, the other in Spanish. The first satire entitled *In Doctorem Damianum Velázquez Satira Prima,* ridiculed and vilified the aforesaid Doctor Damian Velázquez and his father, the comedian Jerónimo Velázquez,

47

plaintiff, and his mother, Inés Osorio, wife of the said Velázquez, plaintiff, and Ana Velázquez, cousin of the said Doctor and niece of the said Velázquez, plaintiff, all of them married women and very honorable and reputed as such. . . . On the second sheet was a satiric ballad in the vernacular, dealing with Lavapiés Street, and in the said ballad many evil things were uttered against Ana Velázquez, niece of the plaintiff, and against a certain Doña Juana, unmarried, whose last name this witness did not recall, and against Elena Osorio, married daughter of the said Velázquez, plaintiff, and this ballad vilified these persons by calling them whores and bawds and other malign names to the same purpose . . . and this witness recognized the handwriting and the style of these poems to be those of Lope de Vega and deposed that he was sure of this for he had many papers in his possession in Lope's hand, and had often seen said Lope write. He further deposed that for about six months he had observed Lope's hostile attitude towards Jerónimo Velázquez, plaintiff, and that Lope had induced the actors of the Velázquez's company to leave him and join the companies of others. This witness knew that various copies of these satires were in the possession of diverse persons in Madrid and he knew likewise that Lope de Vega was a man accustomed to writing satires, and likewise that Lope had told him he meant to do all possible harm to Velázquez and his family.

The Licentiate Ordoñez, about twenty-five, of this city, living at the Plazuela del Cordón, back of Don Alonso de Arcila's houses, who declared that he knew Jerónimo Velázquez, plaintiff, and Lope de Vega, the accused, and that about two months previously he saw a satirical sonnet defaming the person of Doctor Velázquez, son of Velázquez, plaintiff, in which sonnet said Doctor Velázquez was advised not to meddle with the law; that since he was the son of an actor he would do better to occupy himself with the sport of mountebanks, and

49

that he had no need to practice law, as his sister
earned enough for all; that he had not seen the
sonnet which was only read to him, but that he had
afterwards seen the macaronic verses which were
of the same tenor, and which rendered Doctor Velázquez infamous, by declaring that he knew nothing of his profession, and that he condoned the evil
life his sister led, that he was no more and no less
than a pimp, that his father was a pandering actor,
who consented that his daughter be a known
whore. Finally, witness accused Inés Osorio, the
wife of said Velázquez, plaintiff, of condoning the
conduct of her daughter, and defaming her as a
procuress; and further deposed that he saw the
handwriting of the said satire in Latin macaronic
verse, and that although the first two pages of the
handwriting seemed unfamiliar to him, the third
page revealed its form more clearly, that it seemed
undoubtedly to be the handwriting of Lope de
Vega; that besides, the witness had heard said
Lope de Vega twice recite said satire in macaronic

Latin, from which it appeared certain to witness that said Lope de Vega and no other person wrote said satire against Doctor Velázquez and the persons mentioned. This witness likewise testified that he knew Lope de Vega to be the enemy of Jerónimo Velázquez, plaintiff, for in a number of conversations which he had had with Lope and other persons, in which said Jerónimo Velázquez and his affairs were mentioned, said Lope de Vega defamed and abused said Velázquez with words of great dishonor and infamy; wherefore, and because this witness knew and had heard that said Lope de Vega was in the habit of making satires in Latin as well as in Castilian against honorable persons of this city and that he had seen some of them, and because said Jerónimo Velázquez had no other enemy — a poet — in this city, except said Lope de Vega, and having seen the handwriting of said satires and it seeming to him to be of said Lope de Vega, witness was certain that said satire was written by said Lope de Vega and nobody else.

51

Four other witnesses likewise testified, adding tons of weighty evidence against the accused.

That same day, in the afternoon, Lope de Vega was locked up in the Royal Prison of Madrid.

On January 2nd, the Tribunal asked for more proofs and granted Lope de Vega's request for a *curador ad litem*, or counsellor, since he was a minor. A minor was anyone under twenty-five. Lope was aged twenty-five years four months.

Lope did not stand the open fire of the court on January 9th. His arguments were weak. His premises formed no sane syllogism but, rather, fell down, broken-winged, riddled with fallacies.

One moment the handwriting of the satire appeared to him to be that of the Licenciate Ordoñez but, on the other hand, the author of the satire knew little Latin. A few minutes later he was sure that the real author was Ordoñez because the handwriting was unmistakably his and because he was in the habit of writing macaronic verses. When asked to name a few of the Licentiate's poems, Lope did not remember because it was long ago, while at the Jesuits' school, that Ordoñez was known to have written that type of thing.

New witnesses deposed fresh evidence against Lope.

The Tribunal declared him guilty.

He was sentenced to " banishment from Madrid, and five leagues therefrom, for a term of four years, under penalty of having the term doubled for any infraction of the sentence, and also to banishment from the Kingdom of Castile, for the term of two years, under penalty of death for any infraction of the sentence." It was further ruled that he make no satires or verses henceforth against any of the persons mentioned in the said satires and ballads, and that he refrain from passing through the street where the said women lived.

The cell is cold and dark. Carved into the bricks of the walls are hearts pierced with arrows and arrogant initials elongating their flourishes in mute embrace. Dates and words and symbols done with tender or with anguished hand. On this Thursday, February 4, 1588, before leaving his native town an exile, Lope might have written: " A man born between two abysses." But he did not, because a woman's voice greeted him:

" Good morning, Lope."

" All's lost, Juana! "

" You need not worry! "

" That is easy to say, Juana, but I hate to see myself humbled by those boot-lickers! . . ."

" You'd better hold your tongue, Lope! You're in a bad enough mess already . . ."

Juana Ribera was one of those lampooned by the troublesome poems but she was plump, massive and fittingly resistant. Besides, she had no reputation to lose, and she bore no grudge against Lope; she cared more for him perhaps than for her other ten lovers. She was stout, her breasts gave eloquent promise of comfort and warmth; the red carnations on them looked like flowers growing naturally on fertile soil. Her hair was oily and black, so that it was difficult to discern her black mantilla.

Juana and Lope talked about love and war, about Elena and the siege of — London. The time allowed for the visit had been less than that registered by the jailor's watch. Lope gave Juana a letter he had received.

" Juana, take this letter with you. It's from Elena. It may stir things up in my favor."

And it did stir things up — but not in Lope's favor. Juana read it to María Robles and told her that if the Velázquez did not help Lope to extricate himself from this mess, she would take this letter to Elena's husband. It was a very revealing letter. In it Elena said that she prayed to God to rid her of her husband so that she could remain with Lope for the rest of her life. The epistle was explosive with kisses.

María had the temper that goes with Titian locks and she was enraged. She claimed the letter was not written by Elena and that it was all a beastly pack of dirty lies. She tried to take it away from Juana. They wrangled and they wrestled and their nails left venomous hieroglyphics on each other's faces. Juana clung victoriously to the torn paper.

On Friday afternoon at three, Juana was in Lope's cell. She explained to him the new complications. Lope asked for the letter.

" There's no letter left, only pieces."

" All right, burn them right here! "

Juana refused. She wanted to keep the letter as her trophy and to tie Lope to her skirts through this triumphant evidence. Lope sensed the danger and, pushing her into a corner, he fished for it in the warm ocean of her breast. It was there like a poor, sleepy butterfly nesting between two ripe and luxuriant apples. Lope set the torn paper on fire.

56

At eleven o'clock that same evening, a jailor awoke Lope from a sound sleep. The prisoner was naked. He was taken thus into the prison court-yard. The jailor inspected the cell, opened Lope's trunk, searched in all the pockets of the suits hang-ing from a rack. He found twenty-seven letters signed by sixteen different feminine hands. He found a few plays and many poems. There was one, under Lope's pillow, which he particularly liked. He kept it.

Lope stood there naked, for more than thirty minutes, looking into a beautiful sky bejeweled with twinkling stars. It was not cold; he did not shiver. It was good to be outside the cell. He bathed his body in starlight. He felt the breeze blowing from the Sierra. He breathed into his lungs the starlit sky. He had never been so completely naked . . . except once when he had nearly fallen into the river. He had been playing with a country girl on a summer evening many years ago. The stars were shining. The air was perfumed with hay

57

and soft murmurings. The girl smelled of fresh soil. The river burned blue under the stars. He could hear the music of the water. . . .

The jailor came and took him back into his cell.

The letter was never found. But it was considered, on the strength of oral evidence, as a venomous and vicious attack on the virtuous, rightly Christian life of the plaintiff's daughter. Lope's sentence was therefore revised and extended to immediate banishment from Madrid and five leagues therefrom, for a term of *eight* years, under penalty of serving them in the galleys, without salary and costs, for any infraction of the sentence, and also to banishment, within a fortnight, from the Kingdom of Castile, for a term of two years, under penalty of death for any infraction of the sentence.

V

FROM JAIL TO GALLEON

AROUND the market of San Miguel the Madrilean morning is redolent with fish and rosemary, fermented wines and ripe fruits, prayer-books, thyme, unwashed bodies. . . . Lope's heart expands and multiplies itself like that of a cat in a richly feline world. He has been in jail for forty-two days. He now sees the light, hears and smells his town avidly — for he is soon to go away, an exile. He walks intrepidly among push-carts and burros, avoiding the beggars and the ven-dors of scapularies and precious herbs. His rest-less glance jumps over baskets and winebags to linger caressingly on rosy cheeks and promising breasts. With his elbows he cuts his way, passing

59

amidst groups of young fellows who are discussing what they will do in London once the Armada proves its invincibility and anchors in the Thames.

" We'd better take our guitars with us."

" What for? "

" Just to play."

" I thought you meant to give serenades there. . . ."

" No! "

" The girls over there don't understand that kind of thing."

" I hear they're quite ugly."

" It's silly to say that. There are good-looking women everywhere, if you know how to sort them out."

" Yes, but they drink beer, my lad; that's terrible."

" Well, what're you going to do? That's all there is to drink."

" We'd better take some extra winebags with us."

"Never fear! They wouldn't let us. You've got to live on the rotten stuff the King gives us—"

The stentorian voices of vendors and customers collide or fuse with the polyphonous morning.

"Ladies, here's the miraculous powder that will bring home all the lovers ye want! All the lovers ye want . . . WANT . . ."

"Hey, Juanillo, get me some change. Hurry up!"

"Look here, Don Miró, do you think we've got tanneries for bellies? That meat is no good — it's tough as leather —— "

"The finest meat in Madrid, Señora."

"The devil it is! Why, yesterday I boiled it all morning long and my man almost broke his jaws."

"The *finest* meat in all Madrid, Madam —— "

"How's them apples, Joe?"

"What you men need are blankets. . . . When you get to London town, summer or not, you'll be cold . . . it always rains there. Be wise now, men, and buy some of these BLANKETS . . . sleep comfortable among the bastards. . . ."

"What the devil do you think the English women are for? "

Lope walks smilingly through the noisy town. He loves the exuberance, the coarse humor of its children. He enters *El Toro Bravo*. Juan de Chaves is sitting in a corner waiting for him. Juan is a constable, proud of his long black mustachios. He enjoys Lope's company.

"Well, Lopillo, free at last! "

"A limited freedom, Juan."

"Never mind! Spain is big — Madrid is not the only place."

"I say, did you give Ana the right instructions? "

"She's on the job already."

"You think this afternoon? . . ."

"Certainly."

"Let's have a drink then."

The waiter appears as if mysteriously evoked by the word " drink."

" Manzanilla! "

" A double shot."

Juan twists his mustachios with sublime gusto. They are long and sharp like the horns of a bull. His teeth glitter under his cornuted black hair. Lope looks at him admiringly.

" I tell you, Juan, I'll fix you up as soon as I start making money. You deserve it, old fellow."

" Don't worry about that, Lope."

" Of course I'll worry! You may lose your job if we make a mess of this."

" Never mind! There's no mess to be feared. Ana knows the ropes all right. She'll be back any minute. You'll see."

They sip their manzanilla at ease. They discuss the latest news around town — theatres, women, the Armada.

" Lope, Don Alvaro is very ill. Heaven knows if by now he's not dead! "

" That's terrible, Juan! What is Spain going to do without him? "

"Well, I'll tell you — the King never counted much on him for his 'Enterprise.' Don Alvaro is not the kind of man to get along with Philip; Don Alvaro is too hasty, too bold, too violent."

"Is he still in Lisbon? "

"Yes."

"But whom does the King like? "

"Anybody. He wants a man who will obey him blindly, who will capture London for him without firing a gun, if possible. These are not the days of Charles when our motto was *Plus Ultra.* . . ."

A middle-aged woman comes in. She spies Lope and Juan, and approaches them. They stand up to make room for her.

"What news, Ana? "

"All is well."

"I thought so. You hear, Lope? That's always the answer of good people like Doña Ana de Atienza."

"You flattering Don Juan! "

"I tell you, Ana, you're the best woman in Madrid. And Lopillo agrees with me. He'll fix you up nicely. He's going to turn out fine plays with a vengeance."

"Forget that, Juan, and listen. I saw Doña Isabel herself. I told her nurse, a good friend of mine, that I had to see the señorita herself on very important business. She let me in. I talked things over with Doña Isabel, and she agreed to pass around this corner about two. I'll entertain her maids, while you and Lope take her away by the back door. . . ."

Doña Isabel de Urbina, the daughter of the Right Honorable Don Diego de Ampuero Urbina y Alderete, Master-at-Arms to His Majesty Philip the Second, had been in love with Lope de Vega for a long time. She admired Lope's genius and was indignant with the judge who sentenced him. She felt that there was no justice in Spain, that Lope had been wrongly accused by a jealous mountebank who wanted to monopolize all he wrote. She knew that her proud and very Catholic family would not permit her to marry one who, in their eyes, was a dirty plebeian, a low comedian, an incorrigible deceiver, a jail-bird. She was ready for any sacrifice. . . .

Thanks to the clever machinations of Juan de Chaves and Ana de Atienza, the abduction of Doña Isabel went off smoothly. There was no scandal.

Lope and Doña Isabel disappeared from the landscape. They spent a blissful honeymoon in a quiet, dark and not too comfortable room not far from *El Toro Bravo*. Doña Isabel was very happy because she loved Lope, but their heaven was clouded by the news that Spain's greatest admiral, Don Alvaro de Bazán, had died in Lisbon the day after Lope had come out of jail. It had taken a few days for the news to reach Madrid. When talking of Don Alvaro, Lope recalled the episode in the Azores and tears fell from his eyes.

"Isabel, you know how dearly I love you. You have sacrificed yourself to that love. But we must be sensible now. Our country must be successful in this dangerous venture. I must join the Armada! I must clear my name; my heroism shall wash away the vile mud that the Velázquez have cast upon it. We shall marry, your father will then pardon us and get us out of trouble. If I am killed by the English, my death will do you honor. . . ."

Isabel was generous. She loved Lope, she loved Spain. The sacrifice was great, but heroic blood ran in her veins. Spanish women know the meaning of *patria* . . . it is more sacred than *amor*. Both they inherited from Rome!

"In Madrid, on the tenth day of the month of May in the year of Our Lord 1588, licensed and authorized by the Vicar General of the city of Madrid, Lope de Vega Carpio, of this city, married, through his proxy Luis de Rosicler, Doña Isabel de Urbina.

Witnesses present: Secretary Tomas Gracián
Juan de Vallejo, constable
Juan Pérez, druggist
Juan de Vega
Alonso Díaz, all of this city."

Lope arrived at Lisbon in the middle of April, 1588; his marriage took place in Madrid on May 10, 1588. Luis de Rosicler represented him at the ceremony. Lope had known Rosicler for many years and he trusted him. He was a Frenchman by birth and an excellent embroiderer; his hobby, astrology, had earned him constant persecution by the church. He was the lawful husband of Lope's sister, Isabel del Carpio.

Lope, whose parents were country folk, dreamed of some day becoming an aristocrat. His father and mother had come from La Montaña — Félix de Vega Carpio and Francisca Fernández Flores — but since Asturias was the cradle of Spain, all Asturians claimed nobility by birthright. Lope's marriage meant to him, therefore, a bluing of his blood. But it meant more — it was a mighty gesture calculated to poison the life of his enemies the Velázquez. And lastly, he wanted the beautiful and haughty Doña Isabel de Urbina for a wife . . .

VI

A VISIT TO THE KING'S SISTER

THE great day has at last arrived. Philip of Spain is sending his Invincible Armada to pay a visit to his sister-in-law, Elizabeth of England, and punish her heretic kingdom. For sixty years the Catholics of Europe have dreamed of this moment. There has been much praying and fasting for the success of the Holy Crusade.

Early in the morning, one hundred and thirty vessels on the Tagus salute the sun with a volley. It is the end of May, 1588. Prayers, smoke, the smell of gunpowder weigh upon Lisbon.

In the name of Philip the Second of Spain, the Cardinal Archduke, Viceroy of Portugal, on April

25th placed in the hands of the Duke Medina Si-
donia a banner with a Christ on the Cross, a Virgin
Mother and the motto: " Arise, O Lord, and Avenge
Thy Cause."

Lope was in the Iglesia Mayor during the
ceremony but he did not find it impressive, since
Don Alvaro de Bazán was not present. And Don
Alvaro was the only man who deserved to be Ad-
miral-in-Chief of the Armada. But he was dead,
alas, and this Duke of Medina Sidonia was not
qualified for the " Enterprise." The Duke had confessed his incompetence to his king:

" My health is bad and from my slight experience on the water I know that I am always sea-sick.
The expedition is on so large a scale, its object is of
such supreme importance that its leader should
understand navigation and sea-fighting, and I know
nothing of either."

His Majesty brooked no excuse. He was a God-
intoxicated man; his designs were not his own, but
God's.

" If you fail, you fail; but the cause being the cause of God, you will not fail."

Confession and communion were administered to thirty thousand men before embarking. The priests gave each man a bill of salvation purging him of all mortal sin and insuring him admission at the gates of Paradise. Swearing, gambling and other ungentlemanly indulgences were to be severely punished. Scarlet ladies were packed off. In short, our heroes were no daring Argonauts but rather sinless Spanish saints on their way to slay a dragon of iniquity, to burn a viper's nest.

The vessels weighed anchor the 28th of May. Head-winds blew unfavorably.

From the galleon *San Juan*, Lope bade farewell to a young woman on shore. She was weeping. An old woman stood beside her, also weeping — but with anger because Lope had paid only a few *escudos* for the services she had rendered him.

Lope had been visiting them for more than a month; the wench had been silly enough to fall in love with him. She had wasted all manner of opportunities to earn many ducats in a busy season when there were more males than females. This elderly lady had made a pitiful effort to look smart. She disguised her wrinkled face with creams and pow-ders, wrapped the pornographic cardboard of her legs with colored silk. A blue mantilla piously covered her wig, and long earrings swung their emeralds over the paint on her hairy cheeks.

A nasty breeze blew from the north and drove the galleons to leeward. They moved on hesitantly.

Lope took a turn around the ship. The *San Juan* was one of Spain's finest vessels. She displaced over a thousand tons. She carried fifty pieces of artillery and five hundred men, and among them Recalde, the ablest seaman of Spain, a man who had been too close to Don Alvaro not to have learned how to overcome the fury of tempestuous seas and unruly sailors.

For a fortnight the wind blew unpropitiously. A premonition of disaster spread among the crews.

The sun was hot and every ship a stinking oven. The water was undrinkable. It had been shut in casks three months before the sailing date. The meat was putrid, the bread full of maggots. The purveyors had bought the cheapest provisions at the dearest imaginable prices. The men had to live on biscuits and dried fruits. They were human in spite of their bills of salvation and hundreds went down with dysentery and scurvy.

Heavy seas pounded fiercely against the leaking hulls. The ships were scattered by the gale. Some took shelter in Coruña. The Duke sent back word to his King: " The weather, though it is June, is as wild as in December. It is the more strange since we are engaged in the work of the Lord . . . I told your Majesty that I was unfit for this command . . . Now I am here in Coruña with my ships scattered and our remaining forces inferior to the enemy. The crews are sick and grow worse daily from bad food and water."

After a few days of despair, the missing ships

returned. Fresh shoots of hope sprouted in the exhausted hearts of the fleet. New recruits filled the gaps, fresh water the casks, and fresh meat the stores.

On Friday, July 12th, one hundred and thirty vessels set out once more to destroy the kingdom of " fair Elizabeth, flower of virgins." A good wind from the south swelled the willing sails. The prows breasted the waves. Sea-gulls in wake were white words of farewell. Songs floated down from the masts.

Lope is writing a long poem, in the style of Ariosto, called *The Beauty of Angelica*.

By Monday evening the Spanish flags are waving their colors on the English channel.

Tuesday: pouring rain.

Wednesday: rough seas, strong westerly wind.

Thursday and Friday: heavy roll, difficult sailing, ships scattered. At four o'clock the Cornish Coast, punctuated here and there by red dots of fire — alarm beacons. Medina Sidonia hoists his own

75

flag — Our Lady, Christ on the Cross, and Magdalen — at his masthead. A broadside is fired
from every ship. As they face the gray, stony
Lizard, the Spaniards pray. Never have men
implored God's mercy so fervently! The sea is
wide, smooth, stilled with horrible adumbrations
of impending catastrophe. There is a strange
premonition of death. A dense silence. A dark
peace.

On Saturday at midnight the fleet meets a fishing-
smack.

"Sir Francis Drake and Lord Howard wait for
ye by the Sound," the Falmouth fishermen are
made to declare.

And in the early Sunday dawn, the Spaniards
see challenging English banners, moving off Rams-
head, three miles to leeward. The Queen's ships
manœuver gracefully, avoid coming too close.
From their remote position astern of the Armada
they fire with prodigious rapidity. Lope cannot con-
tinue writing *The Beauty of Angelica*. Seven Eng-

lish galleons have taken his *San Juan* as their target, raining fire on her.

The Spaniards were excellent hand-to-hand fighters; they were accustomed to grapple their enemy's ships, then carve their way to victory with their swords and their courageous hearts. But this shooting from a distance was different, alas, it was ungentlemanly!

The *San Juan* alone fired a hundred and twenty shots, but her guns did not carry far. Lope used all of Elena Osorio's love-letters as wadding. He tried to murder Elizabeth's men with Elena's sweetness. But the English were tough; they fired back five times as many shots. The *San Juan* reeled, torn from water-line to masthead, with trailing rigging and angry corpses. The combat lasted till four in the afternoon. The Spaniards did not enter the Sound!

Half-crippled, the *San Juan* followed painfully at the rear of the fleet. Two miles ahead Pedro de Valdés was commanding one of the finest of the

Spanish galleons. He felt sorry for the *San Juan;* he wanted to save her. Valdés' men were sea-dogs, but the roar of the English cannon had unnerved them. In trying to turn back, their vessel collided with the *Santa Catalina.* Valdés' fine galleon was rendered unnavigable, and Don Pedro de Valdés made a wretched prisoner of Queen Elizabeth. The English honored him with their admiration; they brought his damaged ship to Dartmouth and thanked him for the gunpowder and fine swords that they found in her hull.

That same night *Our Lady of the Rose,* another Spanish vessel, was to bloom like a multifoliate rose of fire. The powder in her magazine mysteriously exploded. The air was filled with sparks and darting flames and the groans from scorched bodies. And she sank under a sable shroud of smoke, in a grave of foam. . . .

On Monday the swell was heavy. Men were at work stopping leaks, mending broken gear, throwing the needless bodies of the dead into the sea,

The Spanish Armada and the English Squadron

murmuring superstitious fears; and Lope went on with the writing of *The Beauty of Angelica*. At sunset, the sea was calm and no breeze blew. The English fleet, peacefully picturesque in the distance, looked like a line of cardboard ships glued on a blue sea of cloth. The Spanish galleasses, driven by the strength of oars, were sent to the attack, but a nasty wind rose and Howard cut through the heart of the Armada. The *San Juan* and six other Spanish vessels surrounded his *Ark Raleigh*.

It was then that Philip's men saw the unbelievable; English galleons moving about swiftly, gracefully, circling like birds, all the while vomiting their poisonous fire into the heavy Spanish ships, huge targets easy to hit. Medina Sidonia's proud standard was a pitiful rag; smoke had made of its Magdalen a Kaffir, and Christ had been torn down from the Cross into the briny waves. Throughout the night, divers worked to stop the hundred leaks in wounded hulls. But on the morrow Howard and Drake kept opening new holes and sinking more

81

vessels until Wednesday, when they had to stop for lack of powder.

In the afternoon a fresh supply of ammunition arrived, but the English kept silent till next day, St. Dominic's Day. St. Dominic was the patron saint of Medina Sidonia, the Spaniards were confident that he would help them; the English were not so confident and so they gave the saint, for a birthday present, the pyrotechnics from their efficient guns and a thick garland of hoarse Saxon curses. The *Ark Raleigh* approached Lope's vessel. Then of a sudden, the wind died. She lay becalmed, while, within hailing distance, were three of Spain's finest galleons with Spain's ablest seamen, Oquendo and Recalde. From the rusty davits of the *Ark* eleven boats were lowered into the water. Bold men bent to the oars and towed the *Ark* away. A few minutes later her sails filled with a grateful breeze and she slipped away, a miracle of skill and speed, unhurt and proud, oblivious to the prattling of Spanish musketry.

On Saturday the Armada anchored by Calais Road with its magazines empty. The English anchored a mile and a half from the Armada. On Sunday some Spaniards went to market to buy fresh vegetables, and Seymour and Sir John Hawkins arrived from the Downs to drink stout with Drake and Howard. Martin Frobisher drank an extra glass of whisky. In the afternoon, an English pinnace with a few bold fellows and a light gun drilled two round holes into the hull of the Spanish galleon *San Martín*.

At midnight the Duke was alarmed by the sight of some lights moving from the English fleet towards him, then threatening hulks noiselessly gliding in the dark. As they approached him they burst into flames. The Duke thought they were floating mines. He ordered his fleet to set sail immediately. It was a hurried leave-taking, a stampede, anchors were left behind buried in Calais mud. The Spanish vessels drifted apart.

Forty of them had to face the English. It was a

deadly combat. The English depended wholly on their gunfire, and avoided closing with the enemy. So that the Spaniards were unable to reach the English rigging with their grappling irons; they were doomed from the first. Through the curtain of thick smoke nothing could be seen. But the air rang with the confusion of frightful combat — the crashing of spars, the wild roar of artillery, the devastating fall of rigging over blood-stained men and priests who, crucifix in hand, were helping the living to fight and the dying to die.

Spain's last sea giants were there; they struggled valiantly; with a tragic daring they lived the last golden page of Spanish heroism. Lope, who could have written it, preferred to live it; besides, his lyre was then tuned to Ariosto's strings; he was writing about the silly beauty of Angelica!

The Spanish galleons were torn almost to splinters, the English made sieves of the timber. The scuppers, with torrents of blood flowing over them, incarnadined the sea. At sunset the ship-

Fireships Among the Armada Off Calais

boys' " Ave Maria " sounded like a pitiful swan-song.

The cannons had stopped, exhausted and powder-less.

When next day seventy sound galleons ap-peared, it was too late. . . . The sea had put on its mask of tragedy. Elizabeth was saved!

Tuesday, August 9th, was St. Lawrence's Day. Philip of Spain had once piously placed one of St. Lawrence's arms in a crystal urn in his Escorial. And now armless St. Lawrence could not save the Spaniards from the fatal fury of this storm!

The Armada was driven northward by the tem-pestuous winds. The sea was full of revenge, the sky of frightful curses. The Spaniards obeyed the wind, at least the wind took them away from the English. They were too weary, too sick, too starved and their ships too battered to face Howard or Drake. They sought a passage home around Scotland and Ire-land.

Days went by and the storm did not abate. Food

was scanty; they had to be sparing with the hole-ridden tanks of bad water. They threw their horses overboard instead of cutting them up into steaks!

The nights were long, the days nights. The Spanish galleons passed the Orkneys together. But then fog filled the eyes of the pilots. Some steered on towards the North Pole. The hands of others froze upon the helm; their vessels followed strange paths — grim hulls plowing unknown seas, horrible nightmares of anguish. . . .

The men were cold and hungry and thirsty. They were starving; theirs were open wounds impossible to heal; red carnations of pain blossomed on their flesh. The men were cold and hungry and thirsty and sick, perishing with scurvy and dysentery, haunted with bad dreams.

Lope was writing *The Beauty of Angelica,* and the Duke was writing to his King: " The Lord has been pleased to send us a fortune different from that which we had looked for; but since the expedition has been undertaken from the beginning in the

Lord's service, all, doubtless, has been ordered in the manner that will best lead to the King's advantage and to the Lord's honor and glory. . . . The fleet has suffered so heavily that we have considered that the best thing we can possibly do is to bring the remainder of it home in safety. . . . We are short of food; the dead are numerous, the sick and wounded even more so. . . ." This the Duke signed on August 21st, two hundred miles west of Cape Wrath.

Many ships, wearied by gales and weighed down with the groans of their afflicted creatures, sank down to rest. Others fell to leeward and were smashed up on the Irish coast. The suffering of their men was not yet ended. The natives plundered them, knocked them out with their heavy shillalahs, sliced them up with their sharp axes. The English guards, more pitying, hung them or left them naked to perish of cold.

By the end of September a few thousand dismal souls had returned. They crawled back to their homes, and they died. They were Spaniards and they died of shame, they died broken-hearted. Some had lost the bills of salvation given them by the priests at Lisbon!

Recalde anchored his galleon at Coruña; Oquendo anchored his in San Sebastián. Recalde did not touch his food; Oquendo only stared at the walls of his room. They were Spain's great seamen; they had done their duty. Though they had not been killed, they had exposed their hearts to the Queen's guns. They had brought their ships back to port; their duty to their King was performed. They sat down to die as great men die.

The Duke of Medina Sidonia's ship was steered into Santander. The Duke did not know how to die like a man so he decided to live like a Duke. He was pelted with stones in the streets of Salamanca. He was pelted with stones in the streets of Medina del Campo. The Spaniards all over Spain rained curses on his head. But he did not die; the Duke did not want to die. He had a palace at San Lucar with orange groves and tunny fishing. He was Lord High Admiral of Spain. The King named him Governor of Cádiz and later, after Essex came into Cádiz in the manner of Drake and made a fool of him, the Duke's position improved. He became the Supreme Councillor in Politics and War!

Lope did not die either. When Recalde let go the *San Juan's* rusty anchor at Coruña, Lope went ashore. Back on the soil of his Spain! He stretched his numb limbs; drank wine in a tavern, ate fresh meat, boasted of his heroism, recited some silly verses of a poem he had finished during the trip — a poem called *The Beauty of Angelica*, or something like that, written in the honeyed style of Ariosto!

VII

JACOB'S LOT

WHEN Don Antonio de Toledo y Beaumont, fifth Duke of Alba, became twenty-two, his wary counsellors went about Spain looking for a woman rich enough to buy her admission into the noble but impecunious House of Alba. His grandfather had spent vast fortunes fighting for his King in Flanders; his uncle had squandered his gold in other less political and decidedly less religious causes.

It was, therefore, most urgent to find a fat purse for the young Duke. There was the sister of the Duke of Berganza. There was the daughter of the Count of Oropesa. There was the daughter of the Duke of Alcalá. They all had well-lined pocketbooks.

Early in 1589, when the Duke had just been betrothed by proxy to the Duke of Alcalá's daughter, the daughter of the Duke of Infantado appeared on the horizon, resplendent as a sun of gold. She was exceedingly wealthy; her genealogical tree was deeply rooted in the finest Iberian soil. Some counsellors suggested that business was business and that the only reasonable thing to do was to repudiate the daughter of the Duke of Alcalá. Others brought up the question of honor, saying he should abide by the choice made in the beginning. The Infantado was not too desirable in spite of her extra ducats; she was hideously ugly.

The Cardinal Archbishop of Toledo and even Philip the Second were brought into the wrangle. The peacocks and pheasants at Court were scandalized; all Spain shook with laughter or rage over the charivari. The Duke needed some pocket money. The discussion had lasted for over a year. One day he jumped on his saddle and, telling his attendants with melodramatic tremor, " *This will be a terrible business,*" he sank his golden spurs into the flanks of his horse and rode down to Guadalajara. In July, 1590, he married the Duke of Infantado's daughter.

His Most Serene Majesty Philip boiled with anger. When enraged, he was ruthless. He ordered the bridegroom to be shut up in the castle of La Mota, the Duke of Infantado in his own palace at Guadalajara, and other contemptible plotters to be imprisoned in whatever jails could be found large enough to hold so many. At the time the King considered himself lenient in not sending them all to the stake.

Philip was a very unhappy man. He was sick at heart and his soul grew darker and darker with his cares. He could hardly sleep. He always heard a grim sound of breaking. The disintegration of his poor Empire tortured his confused ears with strange echoes. He prayed fervently at the High Altar in his Escorial. But his God was deaf — His ears too were confused with chaos.

One morning, after mass, the King felt tender —

he pardoned the Duke of Alba; he pardoned the Duke of Infantado; he pardoned the conspirators in the marriage; in fact he pardoned everybody.

The imposing palace of the Albas sat on a smooth, wide hillock thirty meters above the level of the river. The Tormes flowing towards Salamanca crept slyly, limpidly, under poplars, willows, and alder-trees. The valley was wide, fertile and of a varied green; its fields rich in wheat, rye, barley and vegetables. In the distance the snow-clad peaks of the Sierra de Guadarrama and the Peña de Francia pricked puffy clouds with their white spurs. The palace, like the Sierra, proud and solid, defiantly bathed its nude cliff-towers of mellow stone in the luminous air.

The Duke was riding a white steed. He was now rich, and accompanied by many gentlemen. One of them, his secretary, a young man named Lope de Vega, was rattling on with Don Diego, an elderly Knight paying a visit to the Duke.

"This Alba de Tormes is a wonderful place; don't you think so, Lope?"

"Gorgeous!"

"Are you going to stay here with the Duke?"

"As long as he needs me."

"Don't you feel homesick?"

"Of course I do. But what's the good? I can't go back to Madrid for a long while to come. . . . I've been away for ages now."

"You can't complain, though. The Duke was telling me that in Valencia and Toledo you fared passing well."

"Oh, I'm not complaining — but the two years are terribly long. . . ."

"And it's fine living here."

"Yes. At least I have plenty of time to write and dream. There's peace and leisure. Isabel is happy, she's mad about the baby. The Duke says it's a fine thing we gave her Antonia for a name, because she's so much like him. You know the Duke is her godfather."

" I suppose you're writing a lot? "

" All sorts of things. I've done dozens of plays. But my best stuff is a novel. I call it *Arcadia*."

" You're going in for the pastoral, eh? "

" In a way. I acknowledge my debt to Sannazzaro's *Arcadia*, to Montemayor's *Diana*, even to Cervantes' *Galatea;* but my novel is not so purely imaginative as theirs. Everything in mine is true. Every character stands for a person in real life. If you follow Anfriso carefully you'll see that he is the Duke himself. Belardo is, of course, myself. Once you know the formula, you'll see no shepherds, but men in real life."

" But will the average reader grasp all this? "

" I don't care about that. I'm doing a work of art. The public be hanged! I can't write for those who don't understand me because of their sublime stupidity. The real artist must always create for a select minority, for a few intelligent persons, for artists like himself. At times I hate myself for having written so much for the masses. My plays are terribly impermanent, but I had to speak foolishly to fools."

They were passing by a rocky hill. It was a bit of brown stone in the midst of the valley's green sea. A few goats were browsing on the steep sides. They looked as if they had been born from the brown womb of the hill or as if a patient sculptor had chiselled them out of the brown rock and infused brown life into them.

Don Diego knew that Lope liked the " masses," that Lope loved success, that Lope adored to be pointed out by people in the streets as he went by. But he knew also that Lope wanted, at other times, to remain aloof, to emulate the Italians, to surpass Ariosto and Sannazzaro, to be a polished, sophisticated author, the leader of an intellectual circle. For such was Lope's literary dilemma.

"Lope, now that you emphasize so much the question of reality in fiction — why didn't you write something about the Armada when you were in the midst of it all? "

" You don't know why? Just because I was too near, because I was overpowered by it. Too much light is as bad as no light at all: it darkens one's vision."

Don Diego was not quite convinced. He figured that perhaps Lope had not seen much of the storm of battle, that he had remained hidden in a corner trying to calm his nerves by writing fragile stuff à la Ariosto.

One day little Antonia took sick. All that could be done to save her was attempted. Artful healers, wise physicians, cabalistic astrologers came to her bedside. But neither their wisdom nor their incantations dispelled the malady. Antonia slipped away, noiselessly, from the pompous chambers of the House of Alba to the white simplicity of Limbus.

The escutcheons of the House of Alba were wrapped in mourning. Every one wept — and Doña Isabel looked very beautiful in her black gown. She was a lovely woman. She adored Lope and had left a comfortable, even luxurious, life to console him during his banishment. Imperturbably she endured the arrows of scandalous gossip. In her misery she felt exhilarated by a triumphant passion. She knew the virtue of sacrifice; she had seen Lope leave her for the Armada. Her keen intuition told her that on the day of her marriage by proxy Lope was wallowing in the lusty mud of a Lisbon brothel. And though she never read the sonnet in which Lope compared himself to a more wretched Jacob, she identified herself with a Leah keeping Jacob away from his Rachels; and she fervently asked her merciful God to carry her away to Death's other kingdom.

In the spring of 1595 Doña Isabel died when giving birth to her second child, Teodora.

Shortly after her death, Jerónimo Velázquez wrote:

"Inasmuch as I quarrelled and criminally accused Lope de Vega of having written a satire against my daughter, Elena Osorio, and other persons, in the year 1588, and that the said Lope de Vega was condemned to ten years banishment, eight from the city of Madrid and five leagues therefrom and two from the Kingdom of Castile . . . and considering that it is eight years that the said Lope de Vega has remained in exile . . . I, Jerónimo Velázquez, acting as a good Christian and as a humble servant of Our Lord Jesus Christ, deem it well to pardon the said Lope de Vega from all accusations I raised against him. . . ."

Elena's husband was on his death bed. Elena's father sent this petition to the Tribunal on March 18th. It probably killed Elena's husband, for he died the 30th. Don Jerónimo wanted to bring the prodigal and prodigious Lope back to his daughter's bed. He needed plenty of good plays for his theatre.

Lope was pardoned but, perhaps still obeying one of the conditions of his sentence, he never passed by Lavapiés Street again.

Velázquez never got his plays!

VIII

SAINTS, DRAGONS AND KINGS

MICAELA DE LUJAN was nearly
thirty but her body was supple
and vibrant. Her fair, clear com-
plexion, her blue eyes which
always sparkled with strange sweetness made her
look very young, almost childlike. She did not know
how to write, she could not even sign her name; but
she was a clever actress (for women were allowed
on the stage in Spain eighty years before they were
in England) and brought her rough audiences to
tears or laughter by the histrionic wealth of her
art.

In 1596 Micaela's husband went away to the
Indies, leaving her in Madrid with Augustina and
Dionisia, their two only daughters. When he died in

Peru seven years later, he was not aware of the fact that he was the father of five children. Of course, Lope de Vega had returned to Madrid the year of his departure.

But Lope had done a lot of things — besides increasing the family of a man in the Indies. He had served a term in the Royal Prison on a charge of concubinage with a certain Ana Trillo; he had wept at the death of his daughter Teodora, the last bond that attached him to Doña Isabel de Urbina; he had been, for a short while, secretary to the Marquis of Malpica; he had, finally, married a woman with 22,382 silver reals as a dowry, Doña Juana de Guardo, daughter of a rich butcher and fishmonger.

In the latter part of 1596 Fray Domingo de Mendoza sent Lope a bundle of papers dealing with the life of Madrid's patron saint, Isidore the Ploughman. Fray Domingo cautioned Lope to keep " the gravity, good taste and aroma of sweet Castilian roundelays " when celebrating in verse the jubilee of the farmer-saint. Lope sat down and wrote a long poem in ten cantos. Although, at times, sounding erudition and pompous pedantry unduly inflate the stanzas, over them blows a breeze of the ploughed and fertile land, and invigorates the deeds of the saint with the simplicity of the soil. We know that the poem was written in praise of holiness, but the religious sentiment is often overshadowed by the emphasis on humanity and hunger, and ague of body and anguish of belly. There is Spain, the picaresque Spain of rogues, of marrowy folklore and realistic balladry. There have been masters of the brush who displayed as much piety and gusto in painting the shining utensils in the background of a triptych as the feathers in the wings of the angels in the foreground. And thus through Lope's epic sounded the temporal note, and the sweating of healthy bodies is made as sacred as the halo on Isidore's head.

With the same pen that Lope had written about a saint, he immediately started another epic poem in

ten cantos about a dragon — Sir Francis Drake —
who spent his life singeing Philip's beard. To Spain
the English sea king was a prophetical figure, the
reincarnation of Satan. His name was mentioned
only with tremulous lips, and many even crossed
themselves in awe. Lope had twice been to sea, he
had taken part in a Spanish victory and, alas, in
the Spanish disaster. Don Alvaro was present at the
first and Drake at the second. As a man he probably admired the English sailor; as a Spaniard he
hated him, seeing in him only the arch enemy of
the Church. For that reason he wrote a maledictory
poem, rich in vitriol and excoriation — the only
serious epic ever written with the avowed purpose
of attacking a hero. Through it he spoke for Spain;
he poured out his vials of wrath; he vociferated
across the centuries Spain's profound abhorrence of
England. It is a venom-breathing document, empty
and labyrinthine. But frequently a humorous stroke
enlivens the bitter canvas and a genial gesture dis-
pels the academic stiffness.

This poem, the *Dragontea,* appeared in the spring of 1598, but the person who might have enjoyed it most, Philip the Second, did not read it. Philip lay in a truckle-bed in his Escorial. His tumors could not be cleansed and his clothes could not be changed. He was a heap of rotting flesh. He clutched his father's crucifix, the crucifix of Emperor Charles V. For fifty-three dolorous days King Philip remained there, living in death, feeding the green voracious vermin with his clay.

On September 1st extreme unction was administered and he smiled, full of supernal bliss. They all left, and in the dusky chamber he talked to his son as if from a grave:

" I meant to save you this scene but I wish you to see how the monarchies of the earth end. You see that the Lord has denuded me of all the glory and majesty of a monarch, in order to hand them to you. In a very few hours I shall be covered only with a poor shroud and girded with a coarse rope. The King's crown is already falling from my brow, and death will place it on yours. Two things I ask especially of you: one is that you keep always faithful to the Holy Catholic Church, and the other is that you treat your subjects justly. This crown will some day fall from your head, as it now falls from mine. You are young, as once was I. My days are numbered and draw to a close; the tale of yours God alone knows, but they too must end. . . ."

Days went by, and Philip ordered his bed to be turned towards the high altar of his chapel. From his pillows he avidly listened to the dark dirges. When the choristers stopped for breath he begged for more: " The nearer I draw to the fountain, the greater grows my thirst." He bit the crucifix in anguish and he prayed with fading lips for the coming of death. On September 13th, about four in the morning, he asked his watchers for his candle. For many years the King had kept this sacred taper to illumine his last moments. " Give it to me; it is time now! " he feebly gasped. By the flickering light he nailed his last human glance of pain to his crucifix.

Philip the Second was buried in his Escorial. His miserable body was closed in a coffin made, by his order, from the timbers of a Spanish galleon that many a time had sown death among the heretics. . . .

The King is dead! Long live the King!

Lope was riding through the streets of Valencia on a burro. He had on red stockings and trousers, a coat of rough dark serge and a velvet cap. From his saddle hung fat rabbits, partridges and chickens. He impersonated the spirit of Carnival. By his side, goading his donkey along, was a young fellow in black, with a turban fringed with eels and sardines. Crabs and lobsters exercised their claws on the croup of his beast. He represented the somberness of Lent.

Following Carnival and Lent came drummers and trumpeters, and sixteen noblemen magnificently attired — the Marquis of Sarria, Lope's protector, was the handsomest — pranced on their spirited steeds. In their glamorous wake came the fashion and nobility of Valencia, attracted by the splendor of the procession and the unusual mildness of the afternoon.

When the parade reached the square by the royal palace, Lope advanced, alone, towards the window from which Philip the Third and his sister, the Infanta Isabel, smiled approvingly. (The royal personages had come to Valencia to marry: Philip, the Archduchess Margaret of Austria; Isabel, the Archduke Albert.)

Lope addressed them with delicate conceits in Italian, as befitted the character of buffoon he was impersonating, and then recited a nuptial song and a ballad in Spanish. This interlude lasted half an hour, and was immediately followed by thrilling tournaments.

And then another afternoon, in that same square, Lope's allegorical play, *Divine Love and the Marriage of the Soul*, especially written for the occasion, was performed before His Majesty and a very distinguished audience. They seemed to enjoy it, though some, as usual, went to sleep.

Valencia was festively attired. Banners and tapestries hung from windows and doors and there were garlands and rich festoons of flowers covering the balconies. By Serranos' Gate stood an arch, another by the Royal Gate, but the most magnificent one was that at the market place. It was more than a hundred feet high and nearly as many feet wide. Four Corinthian columns supported its three small arches, the middle one being wider than the other two. Upon the central frieze was carved in golden letters:

D. MARGARITAE AUSTRIAE D. PHILIPPI III
HISPANIARUM REGIS POTENTISSIMI
UXORI CARISIMAE, S. P. Q. V. DICAVIT
ANNO 1599

All the panels were covered with allegorical oil paintings. There were richly supported cornices with projections from which hung white streamers bearing the arms of the city of Valencia. Two huge hands, on top of it all, held the world, with the inscription: *Para Mas, Si Mas Hubiera*. And all these towers, ensigns, cornices, vessels, heraldic figures, mottoes, strewn all over the city, were like an extravaganza of exuberance.

Their Austrian highnesses descended from their superb coaches, *dominica in albis*, April 18th, 1599. On ponies they rode by Serranos' Gate on their way to the cathedral. The cortege proceeded in this order: five companies of cavalry, in loose jackets of red velvet and silk passementerie; kettle-drummers, trumpeters, oboe-players in long, full robes; knights and attendants sumptuously dressed, accompanied by their servants in liveries of satin and brocade, with gold or silver embroidered sashes and velvet caps with bright feathers; the King's men in yellow, red and white velvet; four mace-bearers; a few stewards; sixteen grandees; four kings-at-arms with royal banners; foot guard; all by himself, with his usual cane, the Count of Alba de Lista; Don Juan Idiaquez, equerry to the Queen.

Under a magnificent red canopy borne by twenty knights, rode Margaret, on a bay pony. She wore a gold-and-silver braided gown, emblazoned with diamonds. On her beautiful hair was spread a net of pearls. She was followed by her mother, the Most Serene Archduchess Mary, in mourning, and by Archduke Albert, dressed in the favorite colors of the Infanta, blue and white. Innumerable couples of ladies and gentlemen came next. It was a long column, for indeed all this equipage had scarce been got into the forty-one galleons that had brought them from Genoa to Vinaroz, on their way to Valencia. Splendid carriages drawn by four and six horses, all embellished with brilliant trappings and decked with garlands, brought up the rear of the cortege.

The day was balmy and there was no dust, for the streets had been sprinkled beforehand. In the clear air the sun shone down and brightened the whole array.

Lope wore a new suit — he was in the train of

Portrait of Lope de Vega at 40

the Marquis of Sarria. Although he loved glamorous pageants, he was quite worn out. On several occasions, now, he had had to fight for his cape, his reals and his life. Valencia swarmed with thieves and rogues. It was dangerous to go out at night. And perhaps because of the influence of German and Flemish soldiers, a sort of competitive thirst had started in all the taverns. Sober Spain had learned to quaff the holy grape.

In the afternoon the wedding took place. A nuncio from the Pope, freighted with all the robes and symbols of his office, performed the solemn service. Through the rose-colored windows of the cathedral came the sun, to cast its hues over the impressive ceremony — the cantatas of the choristers.

For eight days Valencia was a playground of pleasure. There were cane-tourneys, bull-fights, jousts and flower festivals. For those of high descent there were balls in the palace. For the masses there were dances on the squares, lighted by lanterns, bonfires and ingeniously devised fireworks;

warmed by the lust of flesh, the glow of wine, the curses of drunkards, the flashes of jealousy.

On the Sunday of his wedding the King danced four times: twice with his new wife, once with his sister, once with another lady; but when the second Sunday came, he did not dance at all. He remained in a corner, his hat on, his eyes down, ruminating sullenly over the pathetic fact that he was, alas, a married man.

IX

THE SECRET OF TOLEDO

THE Tagus traverses long miles of dry land. It has passed through the gardens of Aranjuez and murmuringly collected red petals of poppies and white dreams of asphodels upon its crystal back. It has deposited them by the walls of Toledo as it chants an enigmatic psalm. Toledo pushes up its spires frantically in an effort to reach the stars, and the Tagus helps toward the illusion by digging deep into its rock. Toledo is a shifting stage of stone. On its rugged boards civilization after civilization has arranged its own conceptions, its own architectures: the Romans built walls and aqueducts, the Visigoths bastions, the Jews synagogues, the Moors mosques and the Alcántara bridge, and the Catholics cut and polished the rough stone, and tried to raise ethereal churches like a prayer. And all these stones piled upon the rocky surface of Toledo form a jagged mass that makes us shiver, that frightens us.

But there are always harmonious voices of resignation, of martyrdom coming from the bells of convents and churches to console us. The vibrations fill the steep, stony streets of Toledo with soft shadows, with refreshing overtones. The houses open their windows away from the street into their courtyards, like an invitation to repose, to quietude, to introspection. The streets are precipitous and narrow; their cobblestones hurt the feet. The streets are too windy or too cold or too hot; the weather is extremely unpleasant, but there are always plenty of churches and one has never prayed too much. That is Toledo, a city of stone.

From time to time soft pebbles of sound fall into the dead lake of space and agitate it with sonorous ripples.

116

Toledo — Painting by El Greco

By the red conflagration of an August twilight some sword-cutlers were dipping their red-hot blades into the cold water way down by the Tagus. From the terrace of the Tránsito, Lope watched them. A young painter, Juan de Guzmán, was with him.

" Miracle of the water! How its cold caress can make the hard, stubborn metal that glows in its brittleness, flexible as whale-bone! Showers may fall on Toledo and yet its blazing heart sleeps in adamantine unconcern. . . ."

Juan was not listening. His eyes were fastened on the upper story of the Marquis of Villena's house. An elderly man of about sixty stood on the balcony scanning the distant landscape, towards the bridge of San Martín, towards the little wood of evergreen oaks. His name was Domenicos Theotocopoulos, better known as El Greco.

" Look at him, Lope."

" Who? "

" El Greco."

117

" What is he doing there? "

" He lives there now."

" It's not possible! "

" Yes."

" Where does he get the money? "

" Why he's doing all kinds of things. He knows his business all right. It's not all painting for him. He has time for drawing plans for altars and convents."

" But still! "

" Well his son Jorge Manuel helps him a lot. He told me they pay fifteen hundred reals a year rent for that house. Imagine twenty-four rooms! "

" Have you been inside? "

" Yes, indeed."

" What does it look like? "

" Wonderful! The old Greek likes to live in luxury. Of course, last year Jorge Manuel married Doña Alfonsa de los Morales, and you know she's pretty well fixed. She probably brought him a generous dowry and El Greco likes to keep up appearances. And then again he's crazy about his grandson."

" Oh, is he a grandfather already? "

" Already! Why, El Greco is past sixty."

" He should have retired long ago."

" What do you mean? "

" He should have retired after Philip the Second rejected his ' Saint Martial '."

" But what the devil did the King know about painting? El Greco's canvas is great and I don't care what kings or popes had to say about it. . . ."

" All right, but who is to appreciate its greatness? "

" Artists! "

" That's silly. A piece of art should be enjoyed by everybody. Just because El Greco daubs paint all over a piece of canvas and calls it — well, whatever he wants to call it — is that a reason for us to fall on our knees and burn incense to his art? Is obscurantism synonymous with greatness of vision, with

119

universality? That's like Góngora and his chaotic
fantasies. He's suffering from a sort of æsthetic
delirium-tremens and still loves to be called
the Swan of Córdoba. Swan! Gander is more
like it! "

"Listen, Lope, you shouldn't rave on like that.
Why, you yourself used to Gongorize —— "

"Yes, but a long time before Góngora. I used to
call spades ' iron wakeners of the sleepy soil.' I
was a child then. You remember this one from the
Arcadia:

> *If her forehead was not snow,*
> *It was a sky above two arches,*
> *Which, to the rain of my eyes,*
> *Predicted fair weather.*

> *In whose shadow were seen*
> *Two beautiful and azure suns,*
> *Sapphires and precious stones*
> *From these that weep portraits;*

Don Luis de Góngora y Argote

Although from them chaste love
Then made two reprints
That served me for mirrors,
They were false glasses.

" It's either immaturity or madness or stomach trouble that produces that kind of thing. I repeat I was to be excused because of my youth and inexperience, because I was following a fashion of the moment. Of course Góngora belongs in the madhouse."

Juan did not answer. He remembered that Lope's *Arcadia* had appeared in 1598 and that because of its brilliance, bombast, and artificiality the book was saved and became a best-seller. Sophistication was then the mode. One thing Juan did not forget: the *Arcadia* appeared with a portrait of Lope brightened with a presumptuous crest, supposedly that of the author. Of course Lope was not an aristocrat. Góngora knew it; with a cynical smile he wrote a virulent sonnet counselling Lope not to build any more towers upon sand and advising him, now that he had married a butcher's daughter, to replace the *torres* (towers on the escutcheon) with *torreznos* (rashers of bacon).

"Still, Lope, you must admit that Góngora is a great poet, perhaps the greatest in Spain today."

"Yes, he is rather good. But you exaggerate when you call him the greatest. He's probably the most difficult, the most obscure, but that's not saying much. You can make one of those obscure poets in twenty-four hours; a few inversions, four formulas, six Latin words or striking phrases — and the trick is done . . ."

They had arrived at the Zocodover. The square was all animation; crowds of young women were passing by. Lope winked at one of them. She winked back.

"You know, there's more meaning in a Toledoan girl's wink than in any other woman's utter nakedness. Oh how I love them!"

"I like their winks and their nakedness both . . ."

Lope found an excuse to leave Juan. And down the street he went, following the promise of a wink. . . .

When he arrived home it was very late, but his wife, Doña Juana, was still awake — very much so. She complained of excruciating pain. Lope offered to go for a midwife. She said it was not time yet, so he sat by her bedside trying to divert and console her. He expatiated on Toledo's latest scandals, then told her some stories of his own manufacture, and afterwards some adventures of the knight-errant Don Quixote.

"Is that your own, Lope?"

"No, it's Cervantes'. Diego gave me a copy of the manuscript to look over. It's a perfectly ridiculous thing, dull and most uninteresting. Such a bore. It should be sold at the druggist's as a sleeping-draft. Yet you're still awake."

Juana was, in fact, asleep. She had forgotten her pain. Lope scored a point for Cervantes.

He did not feel like going to bed, but shut himself up in his room. He saw an unanswered letter on his desk. And so he wrote:

In Toledo, this 14th of August, 1604.

Dear Pedro:

I'm feeling fine and so is everyone else here. Doña Juana is about to give birth to a child and makes things slightly difficult for me. Toledo is expensive but grand, and moves on as usual, thanks to its native sons and to foreigners. Women gossip, men do business; Justice holds out an itching palm; every one understands but none respects it. Morales performs; the audience hisses; some gentlemen are jailed for it. It was proclaimed that no one should be permitted to hiss. The Toledoans, thus cautioned and constrained, ventilated their bowels in loud disrespect of the Mayor who was present that day. Things calmed down because Morales put on the

boards *The Wheel of Fortune,* a comedy in which
a king beats his wife, and many of those in the audience started to weep as if it had been true. Morales
does not speak to me because he sent me a turkey
and I didn't accept it. I have no door through which
a turkey can enter because they all have been con-
structed for mutton, cow and rabbit, and when there
is chicken, that means, alas, that some one is ill.

As for poets, let me tell you that this has not been
a good century; there are however a few in bloom
for next year; but there is none so bad as Cervantes
nor so silly as to praise *Don Quixote.* The rumor
goes that the King is bringing his court to Toledo,
and this will become once more the capital of Spain.
It will be clear to you now why I'm moving to
Valladolid. I want, may God help me, no more
courts, no more carriages, horses, constables, music,
prostitutes, hidalgos, absolute or " dissolute "
power, nor other obnoxious vermin bred in the
marshes of looseness. Live, take good care of
yourself, get rich, take it easy, don't fulfill your

promises, don't pay your debts, make no loans unless the interest is pretty substantial, don't give a
damn about loyalty . . . and I add no more so as
not to follow Garcilaso's, in that *figura correctionis,*
" I am tending gradually to satire." Satires are
more odious to me than my books are to Almen-
darez and my comedies to Cervantes.

If some one tells you that I write for fame tell
him that he's a liar — I do it all for MONEY.

As ever,

LOPE

He felt much relieved; he put his elbows on the
table; he looked out into the moonlight of the
Toledan night; his candle burned out like a dying
star; he did not move to light a new one. He was
not drowsy; he was wide awake and he was dream-
ing.

That ogre, Quevedo, once said that all we writers
do is to scribble an endless tale of nonsense
linked together with " and so . . . and so."
Strange subterfuge, this tale, to avoid thinking

about the very purpose of it all, he thought . . .
Why do we write? To drug away our days with
pretty lies? . . . So far I've written two hundred
and fifty comedies. I've written epic poems, ballads,
sonnets, novels — Cervantes has called me " Nature's Monster! " Why? Because he envies my
genius. He's impotent, a failure. He said impu-
dently that he writes for posterity. Fine, let his
name be chiselled in high-sounding epitaphs, but
let me get my share of glory *now*. It's today I need
food and comfort. The grave is the same for all, the
banquet hall of hungry worms and maggots . . .
The same power for good that drives me to women,
drives the pen in my hand. I make women happy
with my love, I make men happy with my plays.
And all I need is Eve's apple and a forest of quills.
The public warms my winters with their applause.
I cater to their taste. I give them what they want and
women what they want, too . . . A monster, indeed, a monster of kindness! . . . There's Góngora writing *original* poetry and El Greco painting

127

original pictures. Why original? Because nobody understands them? They look down on the crowd scornfully — they, the *superior* men, the supernaturals. Who told them their clay is different from ours? Their flattering acolytes? A strong dose of castor oil and they'll be saved. . . .

A winged hour, drunk with the bronze of bells and the silver liquid of the stars, brushed by the sill. Lope sitting there at his prolific table, his senses caressed by the murmuring of the Tagus, glided off into the quiet of sleep.

X

THE CHOCOLATE DUKE

THE Duke of Sessa was playing the guitar. His long, feminine fingers plucked the strings languidly and the notes flew tremulously into the dark night. After a few arpeggios, a young mulatto sang. He had a sweet soprano voice and he sang of sad things. It was painful to listen to him; one felt the crystal tone would shatter in a thousand meaningless squeaks. But it did not. It ended in a long quaver, which went floating out into the night, absorbed in the deep silence.

It was now about half-past twelve. But it was still warm. It is by day, when the Madrilean sun beats its fiery rays upon the tile-roofs and pavements, that one expects its furnace breath. But when it becomes dark one hopes to wrap the body in the cooling cloak of evening. It is unbearable to be hot at night.

It was midnight, and the people were stifled in the deadly heat. The guitar had to be tuned constantly, and the strings broke easily.

The mulatto wove a highly ornamented prelude with pizzicatti deftness. His instrument sounded like a mandolin, like a bandore. From the well of his guitar he drew forth tropical landscapes: now his setting was a moonlight night by a lake bordered by tall palm trees; now a serene field, dotted with the red berries of coffee trees, perfumed by the drift from orange groves, bedewed by the liquid cooings of turtle doves.

The Duke, in his turn, now began to sing a long ballad, polished and lachrymose, when a man in a mask rushed in. Two others remained in the background. He tore the guitar from the mulatto and struck him violently over the head with it, clapping it on like a hat.

" You noisy scoundrels, I'll teach you a lesson! "

He drew out his sword and pressed hard upon

the Duke. The Duke ran back; he wanted to look for safety but he had only time to unsheath his sword. The mulatto could not get the guitar-hat off his head, but he could hear the ominous ring of swords.

"My God! They're killing my Duke! Stop, assassin! Murder, MURDER, MURDER . . . !"

"Shut up, you dirty rat!"

"My master is the Duke of Sessa. I tell you, he is the Duke of Sessa, the D-U-K-E o-f S-E-S-S-A himself —— "

The man in the mask backed a few yards and kicked the yelling mulatto in the chest. The poor fellow fell with a thud. He lay unconscious, his head wedged in the sonorous wood of his guitar.

"And now I'll have plenty of time to cut you to silence."

His sword hissed with violence. It savagely struck his adversary's left cheek, ripped down to the lip. The Duke realized the seriousness of the duel — it meant life or death. He drove back with feverish ardor. His sword hit on something hard. He

expected to see his antagonist quail under the pain.
But alas, it was no flesh his blade had penetrated
to. It had struck hard against a wall, impenetrable,
metallic. His diabolic opponent, in open violation
of the etiquette followed by the gentlemen and
nobles of Madrid, had worn a shield. The Duke's
blade broke in two. He was disarmed.

" Hold, sir, I cannot fight! "

" To hell with you! If you can't fight — pray. I'll
slice you up, by God. Pray, bastard! "

It was fierce, the blood-thirsty voice that came
from the relentless creature. He wielded his sword
with unabated fury, striking the Duke again and
again, making havoc of the helpless body now before him. His sword had become a whip, lashing
now here, now there.

The Duke felt as if he had now five, ten, a hundred wounds. As if all his veins were opened. His
blood flowed down over him in copious streams. At
last he fell to the pavement. His assaulter, his work
done, took off his mask, cleaned the blade of his

sword on it, threw it at the feet of his victim and walked away, with the calm composure of a toreador or of a butcher. The Duke of Sessa fixed his eyes upon the now uncovered face. He recognized the Duke of Maqueda.

His left eye pained him terribly. From a gash on his head blood came dripping from his lashes. He was lying on the pavement. He should be standing. Theoretically, he knew how to stand. He knew the operations the human body goes through in getting up. Not difficult. Just the slightest impellent force and he would be on his feet. Just one big effort now, and . . .

The Duke had a confused dream. He saw an immense chamber full of people with long red beards and red pontifical gowns. The eyes and part of their hooked noses were covered with silk masks. He was on an altar, crucified on a cross. A long nail on the left side of his head held him tight to the wood. He had a broken sword in his right hand. His secretary, Lope de Vega, was a white feathered angel. He carried a quill behind his left ear; a golden trumpet in his right hand. He was naked. His sexual organ was erect. He was smiling, blissfully. His nose was monstrously long. The congregation started to pray: " We believe in the all-powerful Lope de Vega, beginning and end of all things, leader of all. . . ."

He felt like screaming. It was unjust to pray to Lope, when *he* was the man on the cross. The adorers went on, imperturbed:

" Glory to Thee, O Lope

Glory to Thee, O Father

Glory to Thee, O Word

Glory to Thee, O Grace

Glory to Thee, Holy Spirit, glory to Thy Glory. Amen.

We praise Thee, O Father Lope; we thank Thee, O Light free from every shadow. Amen."

Then Lope the Father, Lope the Word, Lope the Holy Spirit, uttered in a clear resonant voice:

" I desire to vibrate in harmony with all souls.

Grace is dancing, I would play. All of you dance. Everyone who can dance, dance. He who does not dance can know not what is about to happen."

Lope put his golden trumpet to his lips. He played a macabre waltz. All the people began to whirl around like Bacchanals. One of them took off his mask. It was the Duke of Maqueda. He sharpened his sword on a tombstone. The whetting of the metal produced a tingling pain in the teeth. Maqueda heated his sword in the blue flames vomited by St. George's dragon. He then drove the red-hot blade into him, the poor martyr, bleeding on the cross. Sessa writhed in agony.

The mulatto boy, freed from his guitar-hat, hurried to help his master. He urinated on a handkerchief and applied it to the Duke's head.

" Master, how are you feeling? "

" I'm dying, Bembo. Your poor master is dying."

" Come, master, don't say that. I'll help you. Give me that piece of sword."

" Never! Let me clutch it strongly. My broken

steel, Bembo. Half a sword is good enough to punish those hens and tunnies, those cowards, who go,
masked and armed as if for battle, and strike their
blows in the dark."

"But first let's think of getting home. Come, I'll
carry you on my back."

"My poor Bembo, I'm done for. I can't move.
Look at the blood."

The mulatto tried to raise him up, but he was
not strong enough. He had to give up. He ran
around the square, knocked at a few doors and
finally succeeded in finding a stretcher. A servant
from the house of the Rodriguez came to help him.
The Duke was taken home.

When Lope heard about the misfortune he rode
hurriedly from Toledo to Madrid. What had hap-
pened was not unusual. It was common for masked
adventurers to stab a man in this way.

Lope sat for hours by his master's side. He endeavored to amuse him with jokes and stories. Doña
Mariana also tried to help the Duke. She walked in

and out of the room indefatigably. She brought in potions and pills; with her own hands she prepared poultices and plasters. She made one think of a fish-market whenever she appeared with her eel-like leeches, when she applied them to the bruised flesh, and set them to sucking her husband's dark blood.

Doña Mariana was a strong woman, heavy set and optimistic. By a sickbed she could forget all her wretchedness, all her unhappiness and grief. Her father, the Marquis of Poza, had not hesitated to give her a handsome dowry to improve the branches on his family tree. He had forced his daughter to marry the Duke of Sessa.

The wedding had taken place ten years ago. The Duke was then seventeen, Doña Mariana, sixteen. She did not love the Duke, but marriage had nothing to do with love. She was an obedient daughter.

The Duke and Mariana lived in their palace. They became good friends and they spent much of their time together. Later on, however, the Duke, growing tired of her, began to go out at night with

137

adventurous friends. Often he would not come home. He sought to emulate Don Juan.

In 1605 when the Duke became twenty-three, he took as his secretary the most notorious and scandalous Phoenix of wits, the monster Lope de Vega. Lope was twenty years his senior. In spite of his plebeian origin and slender pocketbook, this Lope had enjoyed the favors of twenty times as many ladies as had he — a wealthy and handsome duke — and yet had had time to compose hundreds of notable plays and unforgettable poems. Lope became the Duke's lyrical secretary. The Phoenix would often lend him overnight one of his obliging bedmates and wellwishers.

Lope found a refreshing oasis at the Duke's. He relished the excellent ducal dinners, well supplied with sherry and malaga, and frequently he was able to give a fuller tone to the hollow jingling in his thin pockets. Lope rode there from Toledo at least once a week and he seriously contemplated moving to Madrid. In Toledo things were getting entirely too domestic. Micaela gave him two daughters in 1605: one, Marcela, at the beginning of the year, and Angela, late in October. Next year came Doña Juana's turn: she gave birth to Carlos. And early in the following year, Micaela brought him a boy: Lope Félix.

Of course, this fertility of his bed bears directly on the fertility of his pen: he wrote during this time dozens of plays and what he called a " tragic epic," *Jerusalem Conquered*. This was a poem in twenty cantos, totalling twenty-two thousand verses in octave rhymes, a sheer tour de force in which Lope endeavored to prove that the most important figure of the Crusades was not Richard the Lion Hearted but a Spaniard, King Alphonse of Castile. Stanzas ran on for miles, embroidering a historical error. Perhaps Alphonse had really wanted to exchange his kingdom for a horse but they brought him a burro instead, and he never trotted a league beyond his domains. Lope took his authorities seriously. They were semi-romantic historians who dreamt of

139

Quixotic adventures; and the result was this scaffold of sophistry. It showed one thing, however:
Lope's Hispanism — his firm belief in the greatness
of Spain, center of the universe. Especially curious
was the title-page of his epic, where Lope was de-
scribed as " Member of the Holy Office of the
Inquisition." The Duke of Sessa had proved influential, after all!

The fertile genius then proceeded in his *The New
Art of Writing Plays* to define his attitude toward
the drama. His treatise is composed in hendecasyl-
lables. And though it was meant to be read before
an Academy of Letters, it was written in a few hours
and it bears that carelessness characteristic of Lope
at his worst. He defended the irregularities of his
art and smiled away classic restraint. He dwelled
once more on a favorite thought: plays are addressed to the rabble and one must talk to fools
foolishly if one is to succeed. A high-brow should
be regarded merely as a fitting resting place for a
hat — and nothing more.

" To vulgar standards then I square my play,
Writing at ease; for, since the public pay,
'Tis just, methinks, we by their compass steer,
And write the nonsense that they love to hear."

Since variety is the essential spice of life, do not hesitate to mix the pathetic with the humorous.

" The tragic with the comic muse combin'd,
Grave Seneca with sprightly Terence join'd,
May seem, I grant, Pasiphaë's monstrous birth,
Where one half moves our sorrow, one our mirth.
But sweet variety must still delight;
And, 'spite of rules, dame Nature says we're right,
Thro' all her works she this example gives,
And from variety her charm derives."

The playwright's chief preoccupations should be unity of action, suitability of diction (the language of ladies must be lady-like, and strumpets strumpet-like) appropriateness of dress (don't let your Alexander run out on the stage in the garb of a caliph, a fishmonger or a Toledoan bishop).

141

Lope's theories were considered advanced. The Academy resounded with cackling protest. Lope was dubbed a " radical." But Spain's theatre-goers insisted on basking in the extravagant rays of his genius. He was a success. . . .

When the Duke of Sessa's wounds were healed, Lope joined the Slaves of the Holy Sacrament. It was a very wise move. To be a Slave meant increased prestige. It all was like becoming a member of a high-class club. Economically, this brotherhood presented the attractions of a benefit society, of an insurance company, and of an Atheneum-Casino with literary discussions, readings, lectures and card-parties.

Lope had earned plenty of money in his life but his pockets were hole-ridden and the reals slipped out into the air with incredible rapidity. He wrote " monstrously " fast; he could finish a five-act play in verse overnight — a deft exercise that brought in five hundred reals. Lope knew that he was getting old. He did not say it to anybody but he felt it. He had indulged in the game of love excessively, and now his sweethearts felt piqued at his debilitation. He did not make them as happy as he used to. His amorous attacks lacked violence. At forty-eight Lope was beginning to feel the dawn of premature impotence. He decided to change his tactics. And so he joined another brotherhood: the Olivar Street Oratory. Among his new brothers were two frightful bores whom he despised: Cervantes and Quevedo.

In the capacity of secretary, Lope attended to the most important correspondence of the Duke of Sessa. He made himself small and humble and useful. He flattered his patron unctuously. " I am happier lying at your feet like a faithful dog than in the company of my wife, of my children, of my mistresses. . . ."

The Duke dedicated himself whole-heartedly to his guitar, to his serenades, to his adventures. He wanted to be a Don Juan, to be respected as a matchless duelist, to be mentioned as a paragon of stalwart knighthood, to be a hero *sans peur et sans reproche*. But there was a man named Quevedo. This man knew that myths and reputations have a common basis — lies. The people of the neighborhood, impressed by the Duke's carriages and luxury, influenced by his secretary's praises and charmed by his clever wit, made of him a veritable Achilles; perfect, therefore vulnerable. So Quevedo spoke sardonically of the Duke's rheumatism and lily liver. And Quevedo was right. The Don Juan-Achilles Duke of Sessa was a popular fiction. It never existed. The Duke, however, chose to believe in the legend woven about his person; he tiptoed calculatingly into this indistinct other self, and put to shame the traditional cat. He lived his pretty lie, and public opinion collaborated with him. People lengthened, interpolated, exaggerated the sagas of their Hector.

Then one night when he was escaping, in his virtuous fashion, the blade of a jealous husband, he bumped into a watchman. The Duke always carried his sword in front of him like a sharp bowsprit, as if to cut the darkness and the wind, to beat his own time, to reach his goal of safety faster. But this time he wounded, or rather, his sword wounded a man. He knew because he felt the impact of a body, heard a muffled thud in the dust at his tracks and because when he reached his room, he saw that his sword had a shiny red sheath.

Next day the neighborhood served up the dainties of romance.

" Did you hear about the Duke? "

" Why, of course. It's the talk of Madrid."

" What do you think of it? "

" He's incorrigible."

" Imagine fighting single-handed against five men armed to their teeth —— "

" But who was the woman? "

" People say she's a very beautiful girl living with Roque, the shoemaker."

" How many did he kill? "

145

"Nobody knows yet. Of course the poor watchman got the worst of it. They say the Duke's sword went in to the hilt."

"Caramba, what a man!"

"A terror, my dear."

Gossip travelled from one corner of Madrid to the other. The Duke was a hero. He had fought five men single-handed. He wounded some, and the remainder had fled. Otherwise he would have murdered them all. A dangerous creature. A monster. Young ladies sighed admiringly, with ogling frailty. Tears of tender love came to their eyes. Oh, to be raped by this bloody monster, wise in voluptuousness, filled with sweetness. . . .

The Duke was ordered to leave Madrid and retire to his estates.

XI

DE CONSOLATIONE

O R

THE BOOK OF CLERKS

Summer, 1612.

TO THE DUKE OF SESSA,
Your Excellency's servant, Carlitos, is very ill with tertian and complains a great deal; he eats nothing. If you have some jelly, do kindly send us some at your earliest convenience.

I desire my son's health in order that your Excellency may have another Lope to love you as much as I do, although he may be of as little good to you as his father.

Your servant, that kisses your feet,

LOPE DE VEGA

The jelly came but Carlitos did not eat it. He was not hungry; he had had no appetite for days. He had no appetite to live. Carlitos was seven years old but his sad little face could have been that of an old man. There was the sapience of a strangely martyred soul within his frail body. It was as if he had forgotten some important toy in the world he had come from, as if the warm, dark, velvet-lined womb were summoning him back. He looked very unhappy and he died, leaving the Duke's jelly untouched.

A few months before, Lope had joined the Third Order of Saint Francis. He felt his own plays weighing him down, burying him in a universe of verse. The thought that public admiration would cease when he needed it most, made him shudder with fear. A few weeks after he had become a member of the new brotherhood, all the theatres in Madrid were padlocked on account of Queen Margaret's death. "I bid farewell to the Muse because there are no theatres. It is too bad, because they helped me defray the tremendous expenses caused by the many maladies that have beset my poor home," he wrote despairingly to the Duke. However, since a good percentage of the box-office receipts were destined for hospitals, theatres soon had to be re-opened.

In the meantime a literary academy was organized by the Count of Saldaña. Lope was elected Secretary. The tediousness of the meetings was relieved by the humorous banter, by the slander, by the fisticuffs of angry academicians. The solemn chamber was often filled with the rumblings and flashes of literary thunderbolts and the Count himself would rush up and separate the murder-bent poets.

One Monday evening about eight, while returning from one of these tempestuous seances, Lope was attacked in the darkness. A sword flashed in the faint light coming from a shop. The man was masked. Fortunately, he was not an experienced swordsman, or possibly he was over-anxious

149

and wanted to dispatch his victim entirely too quickly. Lope became a toreador; his cape waved before his murderer in graceful curves. He trapped his enemy's steel and kicked him with all his might. The assailant pitched head-first on the stones. His skull made a dull thud in the dark. Lope went nearer and saw spreading out around his head a pool of blood. . . .

The Count of Saldaña's Academy expired at the age of two months. Some of its members helped the Duke of Pastrana's youngest brother to found a new one — The Parnassus. And again the literati attended the droll duels of wits. Scholars and poets pelted their bonnets at each other. Lope read two or three satires wearing Cervantes' spectacles, huge goggles which Lope facetiously compared to " a couple of badly fried eggs." Licentiate Soto bit Luis Velez's ear, swords were unsheathed and for a while Martian confusion reigned over the harmonious precincts of Calliope and Eratus.

Doña Juana de Guardo's sufferings came to an
end on August 13, 1613. She died while giving
birth to a daughter, Feliciana. Her will mentioned nothing of importance. And Lope was deeply
depressed when he discovered that all her jewels
had been pawned.

The orchestra was playing something that might
have been a march. There were entirely too many
couples on the floor. It was infernally hot. Drunkards stepped on one another's shoes. Curses and
threats in profusion were mixed with the alcoholic
vapors from their mouths and the savory odors
from the kitchen, where steamed the evening's deli-
cacies — kidney and fish pies.

Lope could hardly stand on his feet. He rocked
dangerously, but his partner, plump and soft, had
become a convenient support, a ready haven.

" You ought to be home praying for your wife."

" What the hell! . . . want the dead to bury the
living? "

The music was tempestuous. The room turned dizzily around Lope. He saw himself once more aboard the galleon *San Juan*, buffeted by foggy northern seas.

" Let the dead bury the dead . . ."

At the age of sixteen he had already been on the road fleeing from death, avoiding the hysteria of women in mourning. He fled from the death of his children. He fled from the death of his wife. It was all very well to compose an elegy or an epitaph, to make poetry. But it was hypocritical to overemphasize the pain of loss. After all, death was often a blessing — it rid men of the burdensome weight of domesticity, of enslaving shackles. Life should be a perpetual renewal. If one didn't die with the deceased person, then one ought to be strong and forget her, to shape one's existence to the life of the living even more intensely. Anything else was flabby morbidity.

The music thundered in a voluptuous chaos. Men daringly unsheathed women from their silken dresses. Everywhere around the Indies — Lope was thinking — this same thing is being done as a matter of fact, in the open air, healthily. Under the gum trees, under the orange groves, naked savages dancing with nature.

The Bacchic revellers indulged themselves promiscuously. Now and then a couple fell to the floor. Their friends would push them to a corner, the fanfare of the orchestra would be enriched with groans of ecstasy.

Lope was wearing a cassock. He examined himself carefully in the mirror. He counted the silvery hairs in his mustachios; the wrinkles in his face. He was fifty-two. But the fire in his eyes was the light of the Satyr. His whole person reeked with ungodliness.

Jeronima de Burgos entered without knocking.

"Pedro promised me a big one for tomorrow. I've trotted all over Toledo trying to get the blasted eel."

" I must have one, Jeronima, and that's all there's to it."

" What are you going to do with it? Give it to Bishop Troya? "

" To hell with the Bishop! The only kind of present he likes is cash. No, I wanted it for the Duke of Sessa."

" Oh, that's different! I'll attend to it."

" Dear creature. . . ."

Lope kissed her. Jeronima was still sensual and attractive. She was petite and plump and she always smiled as if at some ever-present joke she could never forget. She was an excellent actress — her name was famous over the whole Peninsula — and even when away, off the stage, even when about to give birth to a child, she smiled; life possessed for her, as it were, consuming vitality. She used a special liquid to keep her hair jet-black and one could not detect any gray locks. Her coppery skin, fed with almond oil and perfumed ointments, evoked with its lustre some creature of the sea. Her flesh was not like marble; on the contrary, comfortably resilient and cushion-like, suggesting the restfulness of the siesta, or the pleasures of the sleeping room. . . .

Lope pressed his mouth to her full lips.

" There, that's my last mustachioed kiss."

" What do you mean? "

" That I'm going to shave my mustachio right now."

" How silly! " And she nearly choked with laughter. She always exaggerated the comic aspect of things.

Lope stood by the mirror. He clipped off his long, proud mustachio.

The hair fell sadly over one of his manuscripts on the table. And Jeronima recited, with petulant irrelevancy.

> " Let no one say that there is need
> Of time for love to grow;
> Ah no! the love that kills indeed
> Dispatches at a blow."

155

Lope stroked his excellent razor a few times on a leather strop. He was experimenting. He had never handled razors. Better late than never. He must simply learn how to shave. He had a heavy beard, there would be need to handle his Albacete blade quite often. Shaving would become a daily affair. Like praying. It would undoubtedly take some time from his writing. Between shaving and praying there would be a deficit of a whole act in verse. Decreased output. Damn razors and prayers! He envied the monks of the Thebaid — saintly men blissfully content with their unclean grossness to go on lifting up their angelic, perfumed prayers from the cesspools of their bodies. And now Bishop Troya of Toledo asking for mustachioless priests. What a joke! Was the church incompatible with hairy countenances?

The operation was finished. Jeronima altogether gave way to mirth. She chuckled, then laughed aloud. Lope looked different. He didn't look younger; he just looked different. She embraced him; she pushed him to her bed; she kissed him in a giggling paroxysm. Lope had his new cassock on, and his mustachios were gone. He looked so different!

They played at love for a while. To Jeronima he seemed like her partner at a Mardi Gras party, who lay with her still in his mask.

Toledo,
March 23, 1614.

To His Excellence the Duke of Sessa,
Madrid.

Your Excellency, it seems, does not approve of my behavior in this city, of my carrying on the same kind of life that made me a notorious person in Madrid. Your Excellency does not say these things openly, but I can divine them between the lines of your last letter. Your Excellency need not shoot me with this noiseless gunpowder. I would consider it disloyal and unworthy of your kindness to conceal from you any of my thoughts. You may be certain, my Lord, that I desire to finish with my orders, and since I already have the subdeaconate, not to delay in getting finished with the remaining steps. I spend my life between my lodgings and the church. They compel me already to pray two hours a day, and in the evening, while waiting for sleep to come, I chat with some pious friend . . .

And because he who denies everything confesses all, I must tell you that I divert part of my sadness in the company of our mutual friend Jeronima de Burgos. She is now fresher and kinder than ever and pays less attention to other men. Though, of course, many wealthy gentlemen visit her and thus she is able to make money. But I have so little that I make bold to beg Your Excellency to send me assistance, for I have made a fine purchase for my altar, and you shall see it.

Your humble servant,

LOPE

P.S. — I shaved off my mustachios, just to please the fussy old Troya. It will amuse you exceedingly to see me. The ladies enjoy this kind of thing. Kissing becomes a less barbarous performance.

Vale

XII

OUR SERAPHIC MOTHER TERESA AND
OTHER LESS BLESSED SOULS

RIESTHOOD brought Lope nearer to hell. On his return from Toledo in June, he found nothing but unpleasantness waiting for him at Madrid. His job as the Duke's secretary was named by his confessor, San Juan, a mortal sin. He either had to cease taking care of the Duke's love letters or resign himself to foregoing the salvation of his spirit.

"My lord . . . do not be bored in coming here tonight, for I can well speak plainly to so great a lord and master. Since each day I confessed to writing these letters, he of San Juan would not absolve me, unless I gave him my word that I would cease from doing so; he assured me that I was guilty of mortal sin and this has filled me with much regret; I believe I would not have had myself ordained had I guessed that I should have to cease serving your Excellency in anything, and especially in those matters in which you take so much pleasure. If I have any consolation it is in knowing that your Excellency writes so much better than I, for never in my life have I seen anyone who could equal you. And since this is an infallible truth, and not an excuse of mine, I beg your Excellency to assume this labor on your own account, so that I may not reach the altar with this scruple, nor be obliged to plead every day with the censors of my sins: for I assure you that you surpass me as much in what you write as you do in having been born the son of such noble princes. I have never dared say this before to your Excellency because of my great love and infinite indebtedness, each day devising instead, as best I could, a way of confessing myself. Now it has reached a point where no other way is possible. Your Excellency is the possessor of a clear understanding and a generous heart. . . ."

Lope was terribly afraid of falling from the Duke's grace — his financial grace. But still, he hated to ruin his ecclesiastical career so nearly finished — a career which would mean chiefly a sure and, generally, a substantial income. The only thing left was to smooth things over, to balance himself delicately between the two extremes, to prove once and for all that his protector was the greatest letter-writer that ever lived and that poor Lope was not, in the last analysis, essential to the Duke in his winning of women through epistolary eloquence.

The Duke of Sessa, a staunch believer in his own greatness, was readily convinced of all this. His letters probably didn't hit the mark as directly or as frequently as before but the señoritas were dull of perception and noted not his poorer marksmanship.

At all events, a few months after Lope took the sacred vows, the Duke assigned him the sinecures of Alcoba, in the diocese of Cordova . . .

Santa Teresa walked her way to heaven. She was once called the pilgrim woman. She left her native Avila at the age of seven. She worked and struggled tirelessly, passionately. She organized the order of Discalced, or bare-footed Carmelites, but instead of remaining in cool cloisters, cooing her prayers like a white pigeon, she went out into the heat of the streets and the dust of the road. She founded seventeen convents. She governed seventy communities. She saved thousands of souls and it was only right that they should have named her Mother Superior of the order.

Since childhood, when she had collaborated with her brother Rodrigo in a chivalresque novel, the thought came to her that women could also be knight-errants. And off she went, on her difficult errand, knowing that windmills are windmills and that, thanks to them only, white flour is produced out of golden grain. She had no dragons to kill, no chimeras to vanquish. She moved in a world sweating prose. She wanted women to learn this naked

truth and she endeavored to train them, to harden
them, to masculinize them: " I would not have my
daughters be, or seem to be, women in anything —
but brave men."

But at night, after removing the dust of a fa-
tiguing day from her skirts, she flew far into
heavenly regions and conversed with God and the
saints. Some claimed that she suffered from cata-
lepsy. But Teresa went on enjoying her wonderful
visions, singing her cerulean pæans in a pure and
blissful paradise.

Teresa died in 1582, and on October 16, 1614,
she was beatified in the Carmelite church. A sort of
literary contest took place. Lope inaugurated the
ceremony with a panegyric in verse. Cervantes,
Espinel and a great many literary personages were
present. Belittling Plato's gratification at being a
man and not a woman, Lope went on to praise in
passionate dithyrambic verse the virtues and powers
of feminine understanding. And then as a thorough,
cock-sure representative of his age, he claimed that

in the blossoming academies of Madrid there were
many talented figures that surpassed Plato in doc-
trine and intelligence. Lope believed in his time
and in his country. The lights of ancient cultures
grew dim when placed next to the brilliant beacons
of seventeenth century Spain. The knowledge of
his period represented the pinnacle of human sci-
ence and art.

The church palpitated with fine poetry. A sym-
phony of gorgeous colors, the light from the sun
entered humbly, apologetically, into the precinct
scented with wisdom, beauty and conceit.

" Luis, pray what has Lope on his mind? "

" I have no idea, your Excellency."

" What do you think of his paternal worries? "

" Extremely silly. Of course, he has quite
often mentioned a certain Fray Vicente who, he
claims, has entered the Discalced Franciscan
orders."

" I know all that. But still, his letter is a bit

165

confusing. One moment he refers to his son, another to the arrival from Naples of the Count of Lemos. Do you think that Lope is the kind of man to rush down to Valencia in the middle of the dog-days just to see a son or receive a count? "

" I don't believe so, my Lord, unless — "

" A woman is in the game. . . . That's what you wanted to say. Yes, that's the one reason, the sufficient cause, to make Lope leave the frying pan for the fire. . . ."

For seventeen days Lope burned with high fever. He thought his end had come. He prayed with all his heart for a quick death. His body was being consumed by cruel flames and he began to dream lovingly of the shadowy, cool tomb. But his friend Sebastián Jaime collected all his will-power, hustled around, consulted the best physicians and followed their prescriptions word for word with untiring zeal. And Lope was saved.

From Valencia, this 6th of August, 1616.

To the Duke of Sessa, in Madrid.

Your Excellency came very near losing a servant, and if not one of the oldest, at least one who has always most desired to serve you in all things. For seventeen days I have been confined to my bed with a violent fever, so that I thought the end of my life had come; my only anxiety was that I might lose it when I could not see the face of your Excellency. I got as far as the palace, as well as I was able, to see the Count of Lemos, who was much grieved to find me feeble, for I am so changed that I do not know myself. He showed me much favor and had me sit beside him in public. Of the Count I have no more to say except that he showed what manner of person he is by his hospitality. . . . Yesterday La Loca arrived here. She came by sea together with Sanchez and the whole company, with the Count, from Barcelona. Both by land and sea they entertained him with comedies, some of which the Count praised most enthusiastically. La Loca has come to see me and asks me to write to you that here your Excellency has a slave; this is so, and I entreat you not to believe that she was the cause of my journey hither; for I have been here a month, and she in Barcelona. My son is coming tomorrow, most eager that I should take him with me: I have arranged it, although I have lost some of my courage, for he is to be a companion to his father.

LOPE DE VEGA

The Count of Lemos, Lope's former Mæcenas, remained for five years Viceroy of Naples. He had returned now to Valencia with the dramatic company that had amused him with comedies and masques during his Italian sojourn. The great star of the group was La Loca.

La Loca had contaminated Lope with her madness. He had known many, many women after he first met her years ago but La Loca obsessed him. Lope was a man of the theatre, *the* man of the theatre. In fact, life was to him nothing but a badly

168

written play. La Loca was the born actress. Not a woman but an actress. One who did not go on the stage to act things, to play a rôle in a comedy. The boards were to her a natural extension of the sidewalk. Street and stage fused into one concept. She was *the* actress just as Lope was *the* playwright. Thus, La Loca came to him as a ready-made character in search of an author. Whenever Lope saw her he was overcome — not with sensual desire, with creative urge. He must write. La Loca, with her inspiring gestures, with her voice full of strange modulations, with her rich versatility, supplied him with a framework for his plays. She was the incarnation of histrionics; the epitome, as it were, of the history of the Spanish theatre.

But Lope was a poor man full of human foibles. He knew that, after all, his muse was a woman of bitter-sweet flesh. He tasted avidly her lusciousness.

Like a restless Narcissus, Lope disturbed the pool that reflected his genius.

169

XIII

A WILDERNESS OF WOE

LOPE'S axiom was that the easiest way to get rid of a woman was to fall in love with another. His heart swung like a pendulum from love to hatred. "I was born between two extremes, which are love and hatred; I have never known a middle course." A dangerous man actuated by two absolute poles. No nuances. No golden mean — simply two alternatives, one red, one black. Prayer and fasting, penance and repentance were to no avail. Whenever he tried to fly away from his earthly existence, seven dread tentacles always pulled him down and he went back to love and hatred . . .

La Loca tried to poison Lope with her madness. For twenty days his cassock reeked with the scarlet dye of concupiscence. And in letter after letter, he repeated that a fortnight of madness had damned his soul to eternal fire.

Now he *had* to hate La Loca . . . and his heart flew like a bleeding bird in search of a lovely nest. There was Marta de Nevares, in all the exuberance and beauty of her twenty-six years. Her green eyes were cool pools in the forest, fringed with the dreamy willows of her black lashes — pools in which he, a tired pilgrim, had come to lave his dusty soul. Her chestnut hair, curled and perfumed, reminded him of the foliage of young trees covered with tender leaves.

To the Duke of Sessa, in this city, this thirty-first day of December of the year 1616.

My Lord:

I have invited the family of Doña Marta to supper tomorrow evening. They will be here at six o'clock. If you would like to enjoy a little music, you may step in here casually between seven and eight; that is, if you are so inclined and have nothing else to do; and also tell Quixada to send me two dishes of sweets — for that is something we know nothing about here — and also some table-cloths and napkins.

LOPE

Marta was forced into marriage at the age of thirteen. Her husband, Roque Hernández de Ayala, an Asturian merchant, was many years her senior. His one end in life was to make money. It is true that he found pleasure in buying her expensive dresses and lovely things. But whenever she put on her finery, he became unbearably jealous and forbade her to go out in the streets or, worse still, even to look out from the *reja,* or latticed windows, of their home.

Marta could not stand his vulgarity. She tried to be kind to him but her dislike gradually developed into intense abhorrence. At night she would dream of running away, somewhere, anywhere, far

172

from this ogre. But in the morning she felt exhausted, and the action would be postponed. All she did was to purchase a beautiful Toledan poignard and keep it close to her like a redeeming talisman. And whenever her mind, overcome with thoughts of murder, prompted her to take it up, she would repent, run to her chamber, immerse her sinning little hand in holy water and strive to clear her sinning head with fervent prayers.

Lope slipped into Roque Hernández's home stealthily, by dint of his cassock, of his gray hair, of the grandeur of his name. Hernández received him admiringly, courteously, proud to have at his table a " Portent of Nature," Spain's greatest playwright, the Duke of Sessa's secretary. Hernández was a simple man who knew only about buying and selling things and he deemed it a great honor to consider such a significant personage a friend. Besides, his wife talked of how much she was to gain from so worthy a friendship.

What poor Hernández could not guess was that

Lope, racked and sorely mutilated by La Loca, had come to this house for a balsam to heal his wounds, that he had come for Marta.

Cervantes had gone to rest, clothed in his Franciscan habit, face uncovered. On April 23, 1616, he had gone to eternal sleep under a cool tombstone in the convent of the Barefooted Trinitarian nuns. His epitaph was written by the brother of Isabel de Urbina, Lope's first wife.

" Don Quixote " (Part I) was published in 1605. It was a great literary success. But Cervantes remained poor and bitter. Some jealous hack, eager to make capital of the success, had gone to work and published, in 1614, a second part. Cervantes, with his indelible ink, was then writing Chapter XLIX of Part II. This unfortunate event stimulated him to heightened effort, and at last, in 1615, was published Part II — " Don Quixote," Spain's book of books . . . saga of the Spanish soul, filled with ripe wisdom, with peace and secret suffering.

174

Cervantes always wondered about the author of the spurious " Quixote."

The name of Lope de Vega came more than once to his mind. In his Prologue to Part II he declared: " I am not likely to accuse a priest; above all if, in addition, he holds the rank of Familiar of the Holy Office. And if he said what he did on behalf of his friend, he is entirely mistaken, for I worship the latter's genius, his work, his constant and virtuous employment." *La ocupación contínua y virtuosa* — a decently, delightfully sardonic phrase. Everybody knew of Fray Lope's scandalous life and exuberance. *Constant* — Lope the indefatigable; and *virtuous* — Lope's " I have made all my women happy," a veritable blue heaven of love. Lope attributed Cervantes' bleeding sarcasm to sour grapes.

Cervantes would have willingly cast all his novels and poems to the flames if only the public had applauded one of his comedies with the same gusto with which they bravoed Lope's. Cervantes thought

175

himself a fiasco because none of his plays gained popularity. Alas! he was too fine for the crowd.

The wits sitting at Salina's tavern interspersed their literary comments with coarse stories and ribald laughter. Spanish conversation is filled with guffaws and obscenity. Sexual analogies abound. The Spaniard's universe is emphatically phallic.

Góngora was praising El Greco's art.

" He is really the wizard of Toledo. In years to come pilgrims from all over the world will travel to Toledo to see his canvases, just as once they went to Santiago de Compostela or Jerusalem or Rome, to purify their souls in prayer. El Greco is Toledo and Toledo is El Greco. His art seems to have been waiting for Toledo, and Toledo waiting for its interpreter, El Greco. A perfect æsthetic wedding —— ! "

" And besides, the pilgrims will find Toledoan jades here to refresh them on their arrival at the shrine," a young fellow put in. They all laughed. And then Góngora: " I have a few more pearls to

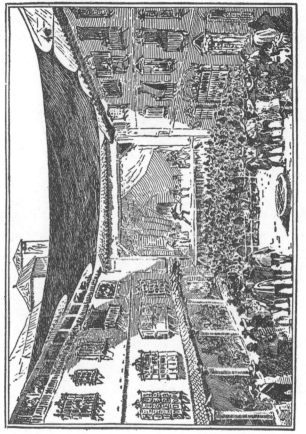

The Prince's Theatre

cast, young man. But what's the use? A country of silly asses like all of you does not deserve an El Greco! "

Lope tried to smooth things over and to flatter the man he feared most:

" Nor fine poets like Góngora."

Góngora looked at him suspiciously, his eyes flashing through his octagonal spectacles.

" Still Lope, I do not exactly consider, like our vitriolic hunchback Alarcón, that all your work is trash. Here and there you have written passable stuff. When the day comes that you will pay more attention to your own feelings and forget the crowd of pigs, your utterances will become worth while."

Lope bit his lips and did not answer. He turned his attention to a wild story that Captain Flores was reciting.

" We had walked for three days under a scorching sun. No wine left in our bottles, and the pampas stretched before us, silent and sear, with not a spring to quench our thirst. Parched throats, empty

179

stomachs, weary bodies and dark spirits. We went on, suffering, leaving some of our men in our wake, agonized, wanting to die.

" At last some tiny lights showed far, far off. We almost thought they must be stars; but their twinkling was so human! We moved on towards the lights, like insects attracted by a flame. We knew they meant water, or death, or both. We hurried on, under our load of suffering and despondency, towards the lights, towards death or life.

" As we approached, we heard the tum-tum of drums and the mournful groans of an exotic chant. Monotonous taut parchments and monotonous sad voices sounding in the night.

" The performers of the melancholy rite saw us approach, but they proceeded with their magic music.

" We lay down at the threshold of a primitive hut thatched with palm-leaves. They paid no attention to us. I became bold and signed them to give us something to drink. A calabash was brought. We poured the water in the palms of our hands and drank feverishly, greedily.

" Yet the interminable drums and zealous throats did not cease. Interminably they filled the pampas with unbounded mystery. And we slumbered, heedless of death . . .

" Morning came, and we awoke but the funereal tune still hung languorously on the air, a rhythmic exorcism that pierced painfully into the marrow of our tired souls.

" In the center of the circle of moaning savages was a beautiful, young girl, lying dead. An elderly warrior, her father, better clothed and with more colored beads than the rest, squatted by her, impassive, cold, immovable, like an idol in bronze. Time went on and we still lay there morosely, infected with the devastating dolor.

" A few hours later — centuries they seemed — there was a pounding of hoofs, and a group of Indians rode in on foaming steeds. Their chief came

181

forward, holding the hand of his beautiful savage daughter. He walked towards the old warrior sitting in the center of moaning men, in the heart of the circle of swaying bent bodies, in the heart of silence and dark song.

"'Friend . . . my grief is great. But I cannot know your grief. He who has the blooming rose cannot know the heart of him whose rose is dead. I too would know grief for the dead rose.' And he drew his knife and drove it in the unflinching girl's breast.

" Then he sat down before the first chief, facing him, while on either side lay the youthful corpses. Now he could know the other's grief, and he sat immovable as stone, while out over the pampas went the same wailing, monotonous chant. . . ."

Lope listened attentively to the story. He enjoyed telling interesting, amusing tales to the Duke. So as soon as he found himself back at his desk, he wrote him a letter summarizing Captain Flores' barbarian tale. The epistle ended with the pitiful note: "Góngora is more human to me. He must have seen me in a better light than he used to."

Urged by Lope's insistence, Marta brought her husband to court. She accused him of cruelty and asked for an immediate divorce. Lope set his influential machinery to work in her favor. But cases like these take days, weeks, even months, to be settled. They are full of unavoidable delays. Lope and Marta trembled with fear and uncertainty. Many of their witnesses refused to appear in court. Marta, down-hearted, considered her suit lost and prepared herself for the cruelty of a triumphant husband. Days went by, and every hour pushed them deeper in the gulf of despondency and dark thoughts. Their beautiful dream had been impossible and now had floated by, like an evanescent cloud of optimism.

Lope decided, in case of an unfavorable verdict, to run away with his Marta. Isabel de Urbina came to his mind. He saw himself galloping away from religion and fame, bound God only knew where, carrying with him his lovely trophy, one of Madrid's most perfect, most marvelous women. But remembering Cervantes' crazy hero he checked his fleeting fantasy. Though his mind could fly, his feeble feet stood on the hard Castilian earth; he knew too well that he was old and that he was no Don Quixote. Jealous Cervantes had called him "Nature's Monster." And so he was. But an aged monster grown ill and weak. His golden wings clipped, his ears filled with applause. A jaundiced, domesticated monster kept in the court's menagerie. The crowd tossing their bravos to him, and he, rheumatic and bilious as an old cat, turning out play after play, repeating his tricks, his situations, his characters, writing greasy letters for the Duke of Sessa, gossiping in old-maid fashion about the life and works of his contemporaries. Lope de Vega, Nature's Monster, Purveyor to the Public, Portentous Pimp. . . .

184

Marta won her case and went right to bed, with the first serious pains of a pregnant woman.

Lope looked around for La Loca as a consolation.

To philosophers love is a desire for beauty. To me, thought Lope, in a letter to the Duke, being no Plato, it is an ineradicable appetite deeply set in my flesh. I cannot stop. Love is a total loss of control, a terrible habit, aggravated by inexhaustible curiosity. I must always have women, but I prefer to go after those I know nothing about. I feel that the more unfamiliar a woman is, the more she will be able to give me. So I am always pursuing some new one. Faithfulness is a synonym for death. I can only grow with fresh warmth. New beds, new odors are necessary stimulants in the life of a writer.

Rather than a woman, La Loca was a novelty. Her flesh was ever-changing, never exhausted, as if some patient but fanciful sculptor were modeling her always of a different clay.

Lope plunged into the delirium of her body, then purged himself with prayer. He confessed and took the host almost daily. A sensitive theologian might have wondered whether Lope went to communion in order to sin with impunity, or whether he sinned in order to swallow more righteously the holy wafer.

At all events, on August 12, 1617, after three days of agonizing pain, Marta gave birth to a girl: Antonia Clara.

The Duke of Sessa accepted the invitation to become her godfather but at the last minute ordered his eldest son, the Count of Cabra, to substitute for him.

Roque Hernández took the new-born daughter off with him. He knew quite well that he was not Antonia Clara's father, but he nevertheless calculated that "where the filly goes, the mare follows soon after." In this case he was terribly mistaken. Mare Marta gradually reconciled herself to not seeing the lovely filly which it had caused her so much suffering to bring into the world. For she could not stand Roque. Whenever she compared him to Lope his coarseness and mediocrity became the more apparent. Lope spoke poetry, lived poetry, breathed poetry. Everything he did or said was graceful and beautiful.

Fortunately death came to simplify matters. Roque had utterly lost his interest in business and lived now entirely on blackmail. Whenever he felt financially embarrassed he dispatched a threatening note. Marta shuddered with fear, but made no comment. Why should Lope know of her miseries? Quietly, with the serenity of Castilian women, she took her necklaces and rings to the pawnshop. It was all very pitiful and heart-rending, but Marta knew that the ways of love and pain often meet and that the best kisses are those salted with the tears of suffering.

Roque Hernández died and she felt more tranquil but not happier. . . .

The sun came in, warm and radiant, soundless music, gay movement of a capricious dance. The rays poured into the cool room like parallel strands of impalpable hair, molten, even gaseous, gold, brilliant light, caressing light, giving to every object in its way a clearer shape, a softer tone.

Marta sat by the window, sewing. She enjoyed making her own clothes, trimming velvets with laces, matching colors, cutting materials and putting them together into new patterns. Her eyes had long grown tired, melting the lovely hues into evanescent shades, drowning them into watery dimness. And this time she closed them. She could see tiny dots racing round. Red-hot pin-pricks stabbed the retina. Brilliant specks of light swirled and clashed. Marta felt like shouting, like crying for help; the pain was so intense, so piercing that it took her breath away.

She opened her lids. Her open eyes saw nothing but bright motes of color against a pitch-black background. Gradually the restless specks lost their

188

power. They died out, one by one, like dying stars. The world went back into a womb of black chaos; full of sound and movement, but with no color, no shape, no light.

Marta remained submerged in shadow. Amaurosis. Sudden blindness without cause. No illness, no lesion. Just darkness.

While skillful doctors tried, with plasters and ointments, to rescue Marta from her clinging night, Lope's daughter Marcela waited, too, for a miracle. She watched for an angel of her Lord who would come bearing to her cell at the convent rays of the sun, clusters of sunshine for Marta's eyes. Marcela had joined the sisterhood of the Barefooted Trinitarians. Lope suffered at her decision but he dared not interfere. She had been his confidante and amanuensis. Now she was collecting and chronologically classifying his love letters to La Loca, now she was taking a play or a passionate message by dictation, now she was correcting a comedy written in too great haste.

189

Marcela was a poetess besides — and a good one at that. Lope always referred approvingly to her work. But she was pretentious and vain. Lope's epistles to the Duke of Sessa contained generally a short but pointed postcript such as " Don't forget to send Marcela twenty yards of taffeta," or " Marcela needs some silk stockings " — brief testimonies to her feminine preoccupations. But now Marcela besprinkled the bare, white walls of her cell with her proud blood; she wanted to crush her vanity, to blot out her mortal sins. She prayed and fasted and punished herself, and asked the Madonna for a few rays of beneficent light for Marta's beautiful, green eyes.

The sky of Madrid, the deliquescent blue of a winter Sunday. A blast of cold wind coming from the Sierras blew the black baize hangings at the windows. In the streets swarmed the people, dressed in mourning. Farmers and shepherds had come from distant places — some had walked for a whole week, covered scores of miles — to be present at this solemn occasion: the burning at the stake of Benito Ferrer.

A Catalonian by birth, Benito Ferrer had been a Barefooted Franciscan for eight months and then a Barefooted Carmelite for six. He had been expelled from both orders. For twelve years he had tramped over France, Ireland, Flanders, Naples, begging alms, pretending to be a priest, but without ever going to mass or confession.

On his arrival at Madrid, the Vicar ordered his imprisonment. One day, while attending mass at the chapel of the jail, "agitated by a diabolical fury," he snatched the consecrated host from the hands of the celebrant and destroyed it.

For two years and four months he remained in Toledo locked in a secret dungeon of the Inquisition. His friends tried to prove that Ferrer was a lunatic and that he was not responsible for his actions. But the Grand Inquisitor Gonzalo Chacon set his legal machinery to work and it was ascertained *nemine dissentiente* that Ferrer not only was and always had been sane, but that he was also:

Primo: the son of a Jewish woman

Secundo: a staunch Lutheran

Tertio: a fervent Calvinist

Quarto: a sacrilegious and blasphemous beast

Quinto: a son of Satan

On Sunday, January 21st, 1624, Catholic Spain, dressed in black, moved on, firm in its faith, towards the Puerta de Alcalá where the Inquisition's stand broke the monotony of black hangings and prayers with its thrones of scarlet and the emblems of the Holy Office and the King, embroidered in silver thread. In the center of the plaza was a little altar under the shadow of a huge green cross covered with a black veil blown back by the wind. And twelve big torches twinkling, waiting . . .

All the bells of Madrid's churches cast out their melancholy tolling over the city as the procession moved along slowly, carried away with its mourning and religious fervor. First came the guards of the Holy Office, with swaying panaches, clinking chains and shining halberds, marking time. Then friars in cassocks of brown, white or black, sandalled or barefooted, their banners and standards raised amid the heavy clouds flowing from silver censers and the monotonous chanting of Latin. Next the grandees, in double file, ceremonious and proud in their black velvet and white ruffs, slender and quixotic, with burning eyes and pointed beards, like the tragic phantoms in " The Burial of the Count Orgaz "; dignitaries of the church, benign under their heavy mitres, sprinkling the bystanders with their holy hyssops; and then a violent purple note, stiff and terrifying, the Grand Inquisitor.

Ten or fifteen penitents followed with heads uncovered, bent with grief and shame, holding in their right hand an unlighted candle. They had confessed and repented, and they walked slowly toward the altar, to be converted to or to be reconciled with the Only True Faith. Varicolored crosses painted on their yellow cloaks declared in full the nature of their sins and the knots on the rope around their neck foretold the number of lashings they were to receive.

Pages in black carried, on top of long green poles, figures of straw — grotesque images upon which Inquisitional justice was to fall in the absence of the flesh and bone culprits, clever fellows who had saved themselves by escaping to other countries.

And then, guarded each by two intendants of the Holy Office and four soldiers, the graceless sinners on their way to the stake, each wearing the tragic sanbenito and yellow pasteboard coronet, decorated with flames and demons.

A gruff and hissing mass of people walked behind them. They were not allowed to touch the penitents but, instead, kept up their stridulous stream of curses and insults.

When they neared the Puerta de Alcalá the crowd stampeded; everyone wanted to have a look. The best seats on the stand were reserved for the clergy and nobility, but the populace percolated into all other vacant corners.

Vendors boisterously cried their refreshments about the stand — Valencia oranges, codfish fritters, cheap wines, figs, fried pork, Malaga grapes, oysters on the half shell.

People ate and drank, gossiped and made merry as if at a dance or bullfight. They were very particular spectators, difficult to please. They cared nothing about edicts or technicalities intoned in the monotonous Latin of a bearded reader. Even lashings and minor tortures did not interest them. These were light numbers, preliminaries before the *pièce de résistance*. To keep off boredom they kept to their careless, gay talk of wine, women and the current bullfights. The younger set punctuated their munching of dried fruit and fried pork with sonorous kisses and boisterous guffaws.

But when the great culprits, hoisted to their poles, stood erect, clamped to iron rings, the crowd quieted down like a subdued sea. The well-paid

195

executioners carefully selected their wood, piling around each stake logs green or dry according to the penitent's offense . . . gross execution-ers feeding their fires of suffering with all the care of persons feeding delicate animals of different species. Huge bellows roused the logs into hysteric cracklings and Dominican friars with ivory cruci-fixes moved around looking into the glassy stares of the penitents.

Benito Ferrer was bound to his post with heavy chains. Around his scaffold tongues of flame began to lick. It was the language of green timber burn-ing. The air gave off an odor of resin and boiling sap. Ferrer's eyes bulged and the crowd was avid for more. His beard was licked off by a driving tongue of flame. Held fast by the great chains he writhed and twisted in an agony of living Purga-tory, as first the skin was burned, then the flesh seared by the horrid flames. The joy of the specta-tors would be momentarily broken as the increas-ing smoke would belch forth and hide or distort

196

An Act of Faith

the suffering body. Only one man could have painted the scene, one who knew the secret of torture and contortion — Domenicos Theotocopoulos, El Greco.

The Puerta de Alcalá reeked with the stench of burning flesh. The crowd, elated, drunk with the suffering of others, drank it in avidly. This was what they liked — the more horrible the suffering, the more successful their day. Catholic Spain enjoyed these autos da fé and celebrated the triumphs of the One True Faith.

Lope, Familiar of the Holy Office — a title he loved to place after his name on the title page of his books — saw *his* country revelling in torture, gloating over the sweets of pain. He knew his Spain, and he was sure that after these bloody, nerve-racking pageants — flapping of deathly wings among agonized, pale Christs, blood, prayers and lurid flames mingling in a man-made Day of Judgment — the crowd required a dose of healthy laughter, a fugue of comedy and hilarity. Spain too well knew real tragedy to have playwrights try their hand at it on the stage, and Lope's secret, the secret of his great success, was the happy ending. Calderón was then twenty-four and his preoccupation was exquisite poetry about shepherds and saints.

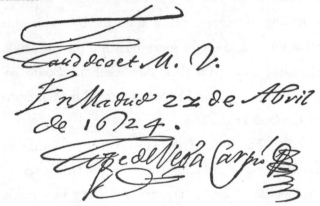

Lope de Vega's Signature, on the Original Copy of His Play, El Marqués de las Navas

On June 29, 1625, Lope entered the Congregation of Saint Peter, an order composed of priests born in Madrid. " Every day he visited for purposes of prayer and supplication the sanctuary of Atocha, and frequently exercised his sacred ministry in the hospitals, consoling and serving the sick with pious and charitable zeal. . . ."

Marta's mind became like a dark attic inhabited by terrifying specters. She could see rain falling torrentially over the Castilian wasteland. Water on sear earth. Steam diaphanous as mist. Spare reeds growing up like the arms of emaciated corpses. Roque, her husband, had been vomited from the belly of a monstrous crocodile. Green Roque covered with bile, spitting blood, rushing toward her, with two murderous horns sticking out from his forehead, holding an ass's jawbone in his right hand. Suddenly he stopped and with the long, sharp claws of his left hand ripped a piece of his own flesh and roasted it carefully by the flame coming from the burning corpse of a victim of the Inquisition. Marta screamed desperately. Her voice echoed and re-echoed emptily, with the hollowness of insane voices. She was mad! Blind of eye and mind; submerged in fearful dark, visually and mentally.

Marta's tragedy left deep scars on Lope. He grew hypochondriac. Unaffected by his frequent successes, he ceased to brag about his greatness. Men applauded and petted him; used *Lope* as an adjective of excellence, a synonym for perfect or stunning: " a Lope diamond," " a Lope day," " a Lope carriage," " a Lope woman," or " She is quite Lope." But Lope's sadness increased with Marta's suffering and raving; with her nails she had disfigured her beautiful face and torn to shreds her most exquisite gowns.

Lope sang mournfully about " Death taking revenge on Love." It was, indeed, as if the dark hand of Death had stealthily stolen the light from Marta's eyes; and, not satisfied with that, had muddled her brains into a demoniacal madness. Only Death could have dared spoil so lovely a creature.

Lope prayed and prayed. And the walls of his little room were daily sprinkled with the blood of his penance. Marcela also prayed and wore rough, pricking burlap under the clothes that covered her martyred body, till Marta awoke one day with a clear mind. She spoke with restraint and poise. But her sanity pained her too much because her tremulous hands no longer caressed a young, sound body but one aged and faded, scarred with too much suffering.

Spring was approaching; the garden bloomed with perfume and the shrubs with winged song. But the shadows in her face grew deeper. She was dead.

XIV

TWO CROSSES

LOPE had lost many of his children. But they died while very young and it had not grieved him so much as when he saw his beloved daughter Marcela enter the convent or his rebellious son Lope Felix go to sea.

And now in 1633 another of his daughters, Feliciana, married Luis de Usategui, a clean-cut, honest fellow with a high-sounding position but a meager salary: Luis de Usategui, "Oficial de la Secretaría del Real Consejo de la provincia del Pirú, en el oficio del Señor Don Fernando Ruiz de Contreras, del Consejo de Su Majestad y su Secretario en el dicho Real Consejo de las Indias." To keep up appearances Lope furnished his daughter with a dowry of five thousand ducats and a magnificent trousseau.

So Antonia Clara, his youngest, his pet daughter, became his one great solace. He was an old man in his seventies; she a girl of seventeen, charming as Doña Marta and just as beautiful. Proud of her youth and freshness, proud of her father's glory, she spent long hours in front of her silvery mirror. She wanted to look blasé and mature. Her greatest delight consisted of beautifying herself by drawing kohl circles under her clear, green eyes, by carefully picking her eyebrows, by curling her lashes, by softening her skin with diverse ointments.

Antonia Clara accompanied her father to rehearsals and shows. She liked applause and flattery. She mixed a great deal with actors and acquired the worldly vocabulary of that crowd. In fact, it was not merely a question of words, she loved to be kissed furtively behind convenient curtains. From mere oral she had moved on to actual osculatory performances.

One day Don Enrique Felipez de Guzmán, the bastard son of the Count-Duke of Olivares, cast his expert eyes over her and found her deliciously ripe for more advanced practices. He easily convinced Antonia Clara that her father, a vainglorious rather dilapidated priest, could not give her the rich garments and exquisite jewels she so well deserved, but that he, well on his way to become Spain's most powerful personage, stood ready to sacrifice his life and his fortune to her beauty.

The young girl's head reeled in the smoke of infatuation. She saw herself countess and duchess, dressed in magnificent gowns, more radiant in her youth than the brilliant stones adorning her fingers, her arms, her neck, her ears, her hair.

And in a few days she was gone, carrying in her wake all her belongings and her faithful maid.

"Like the tree, the fruit," Lope exclaimed bitterly. The old poet in contrition sank down into pained silence. His life of Don Juan passed through his mind. Antonia Clara was the daughter of two great sinners: Marta and Lope. Marta's blindness, insanity and death was the price of her guilt. And now came his turn. A seventy-year-old man walking alone in a wasted orchard. All his great loves had flown; he, alone in his cold glory. No one with whom to share it. It was too burdensome for his feeble body to stand. Fame that kills in a deserted garden . . .

The sails hung drowsily from the yards. The wind had gone to rest yonder on Margarita Island, far away from Venezuela, amid the palms animated with the colors and sounds of tanagers, parrots and monkeys. The sea was ominously calm and silent. Only the sunset singing a splendid hosanna of brilliant hues. And the men lying on the decks, talking among themselves, waiting for the wind to blow. For weeks and weeks they had sailed. Their beards were salty with the brine, their souls rusty with the sea.

"Wait, Lope, and you shall see pearls bigger than hazel nuts."

An old sea-dog, way on in his eighties, talking at sunset of pearls bigger than hazel nuts.

"Yes, years ago, in 1579, many years before your birth — I was then half your age — we brought our great King Philip the Second a huge one . . . two hundred and fifty karats. . . . And His Majesty thanked us in person, and we drank some of his own wine . . . and we were happy, we fishermen, drinking a king's wine. So back we went to fish for pearls but we have never found another worthy of a sovereign. Perhaps this time we will be luckier."

Lope de Vega's son, Lope Felix, listened to the old mariner. Lope Felix regretted he had not thought long before of going to sea as a fisherman. He had fought the Dutch and the Turks, he had helped the Marquis de Santa Cruz — Don Alvaro de Bazán's son — in many victories. He had risen from simple sailor to ensign and was about to be promoted to captain. But somehow he would have preferred to have always sailed with this old fisherman who knew the secrets of the sea, who piloted his vessel by the stars, whose highest dream was to bring a pearl the size of a hazel nut to a king and drink a goblet of royal wine.

The glamour of sunset faded into the deliquescent hues of twilight. And the whisperings of the fishermen dimmed into soft murmurings. The wind asleep on Margarita Island, where the parrots and monkeys went on saying strange things in their wise gibberish.

And then night came down suddenly, like the pouring of black ink over the sky. And with the night, wind, surge. Full sails. Rocking and rolling. Then thunder. Violent flashes of lightning. Heavy rain pouring torrentially, nearly horizontally, like a liquid wind. Gigantic waves lashing the craft, a mere nut-shell. The old sea-battered sailors knew the fury of tropical storms. They smiled wisely, like husbands who know too well the whims of their shrewd wives. They poured rum into their stomachs; they went driving through angry seas; the men sang rollicking, bawdy songs.

Lope Felix felt elated. These men of the sea infected him with their exuberant joy. He thought of his father controlling a country. Five different comedies in Madrid wildly applauded the same night by lords and merchants, publicans and poets, priests and prostitutes. Lope de Vega, Nature's Monster, Phoenix of Wits, sailing through the uncharted sea of passions and emotions, like these men, playing with storms. . . .

Theirs was a tight little craft. Let the wind blow with all its fury, the waves pile up high as they might, they would see the storm through. And they went back — far too many of them — to their drinking and singing.

Three vivid flashes in the sky. There, over the bow, look-out and captain saw a low-lying reef, arms outstretched. Quick commands, helm thrown

TWO CROSSES

over — but too late. Too late, for nothing could have averted the smash. . . .

Drowned in their prison like rats was their fate. Down they sank to sleep an eternal sleep on floors carpeted with pearls of unbelievable karats, with pearls that kings will never see.

" I cannot bear these two crosses," Lope uttered feebly. He felt too weak to stand any more suffering — Antonia Clara's abduction, Lope Felix's unknown death: two crosses, one upon each shoulder, for him who could hardly carry the wreaths of his triumphs.

Alonso Pérez, publisher and bookseller, had always endeavored to do his best to help Lope both financially and spiritually. He edited and printed several of Lope's works and frequently loaned him money. He paid eight ducats for Marta's funeral. Now Don Alonso tried to cheer the tristful bard. He invited Lope to dinner on August 6, 1635, the day of the Transfiguration.

Alonso's son, the promising writer Juan Pérez

209

de Montalván, completed the trio. The three men ate quietly. All attempts at good humor and gayety were chilled by Lope's sombre complaints.

"I feel so depressed. My heart is breaking, slowly, bit by bit, and I pray God to shorten my life."

"But my dear Lope, you should not keep harping on your suffering. Learn to forget! You look strong enough, and I would not be surprised if twenty years from today the rôles will be turned around and you will be consoling me instead."

"May God have pity on me, Alonso."

The days went by and Lope's life was like a poem of austerity and saintliness. Every morning, before sunrise, after saying mass in his oratory, he watered the plants of his little garden. He did it humbly, seeing and worshipping God in every flower, in every pistil and petal. His eyes were growing weaker, and he was served with meat every day, including Friday; but Lope refused, and tasted none of it, and the whitewashed walls of his room, sprinkled with blood, day by day registered the scarlet notes of his penance. His body weighed on him, as much as the ill-smelling carcass of his muddy past. He now thought only about the purification of his soul — cleansing it with incense and prayer.

Lope fainted and fever consumed him. They bled him three, four, five times. When, on Sunday, his friend, Dr. Negrete, physician to His Majesty, took his pulse and heard the strange rattling in his chest, he called for the sacrament.

" It relieves those who are to die and helps those who are to recuperate . . ."

" My hour is near then, thanks be to God for his mercy," Lope sighed happily.

The viaticum came and Lope wept with joy. He gave his blessings to his daughter Feliciana and begged the Duke of Sessa to be her guardian. He bade farewell to all his friends, to all the great writers of Madrid.

" I would exchange all the applause that was

211

showered on me during my career as a playwright, for the performance of just one more virtuous act. . . . The only purpose in life is to be good. . . ."

The gentlemen in black, in the sad room, focussed their tearful glances on the great Lope de Vega. And because they were Spaniards, knowing all about the mystery of Ascension, they were not surprised to see Nature's Monster rise from the slime of a sinful past to the saintliness of heaven.

Lope spent a restless night, pursued by the evil imaginings of his conscience.

Monday dawned full of suspense. His existence swung dangerously from life to death, from death to life in a sustained agony. In the afternoon, at five fifteen, he kissed his crucifix. Friendly voices invoked the names of Jesus and Mary, and Lope smiled, and drew his last breath. . . .

The 27th day of the month of August, in the year of Our Lord 1635, Fray Lope Félix de Vega Carpio, was dead. He had attained the age of seventy-three. He had written twenty-two hundred plays of at least three thousand verses each, five epic poems, many eclogues, romances, sacred poems, sonnets, epistles, burlesque poems, two romances in prose and a collection of novels. Over twenty-two million three hundred-thousand lines, upon a hundred and thirty thousand two hundred and twenty-two sheets of paper. He left as many lines unwritten. . . . R.I.P. Amen.

The funeral was a most solemn and imposing ceremony. All Madrid was there, weeping for a prodigious son. And with Madrid, all Spain. The Phoenix was dead; the theatres closed; the churches echoed with requiem masses.

The cortège formed at Francos Street, and filed slowly along San Agustin Street towards Cantarranas Street. It was a detour. But Sor Marcela had begged the Duke of Sessa to let her see her father's funeral. And the black box, buried in wreaths, passed amid tears, in front of the convent of the Barefooted Trinitarians. Sor Marcela prayed and cried bitterly, and some of the nuns suspected that she was more than a " distant relative " of the deceased. The cortège went on along Leon Street and the Plazuela de Anton Martin, through Atocha Street into the church of San Sebastian.

Requiem mass. Tall yellow candles around a coffin. A smell of melting wax and incense, of flowers and mourning. Fray Francisco de Peralta stands before the assembled friends of the dead man. He tells how from very infancy that supreme and virtuous spirit, Lope de Vega, was bent upon a life of guiding, tutoring, preserving humankind, upon averting even the most trifling sin. Some members of the audience smile, in spite of their grief. But they do not protest. Myth has started to weave its perfect and beautiful lie.